GRAND NATIONAL
— AINTREE —

THE GRAND NATIONAL

AINTREE'S OFFICIAL ILLUSTRATED HISTORY

Reg Green

Virgin

CONTENTS

INTRODUCTION

Like most of my generation, life as a child in Britain during the early 1940s was a mixture of confusion, fear and uncertainty: confused as to why war should mean that so many fathers were away from home; fearful of the nightly screech of the air raid siren; uncertain if there could ever be a time when a normal, carefree way of life could be ours.

Living in a Liverpool battle-scarred through regular poundings by Hitler's Luftwaffe, our city seemed a drab, cheerless place. Our principal pastime was the rather gruesome practice of searching for and collecting shrapnel from the mounds of rubble which was all that was left of so many homes. To our immature ears the names Dunkirk, El Alamein and Pearl Harbour sounded mysteriously grand and we felt sure they were important because they seemed often on the lips of grown-up people. But on reflection, I can now feel much sympathy for the overworked men and women who tried so hard to teach us school work, for we must surely have been the most frustrating group of children they had ever come across. Learning the three Rs was the furthest thing from our minds, our level of attention was minimal and despite the ceaseless efforts of the teachers, we showed no interest at all in the rudiments of education.

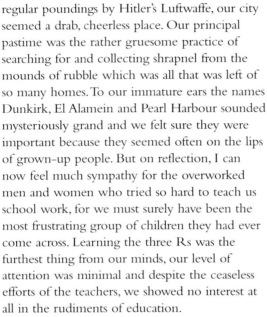

For me everything changed one Sunday afternoon in 1943, when my father took me on a tram ride from Everton Valley to the Sefton Arms terminus at Aintree. It was the furthest I'd ever been from the centre of Liverpool where we lived and although unfamiliar with the area, it felt a strangely tranquil place. Strolling for the first time down an avenue I was soon to know as the Melling Road, we suddenly left the superior looking houses behind us to miraculously enter a vast expanse of open countryside and it was here the my dad spoke the words which were to change my life forever. He said simply, almost casually but in what I now remember as a confiding manner, 'This is the home of the Grand National'.

It was either the words themselves or the way they were delivered which immediately aroused my attention. Hanging on his every word, I listened intently as he continued, telling the most fascinating tales of the races he had witnessed on that historic turf and explaining why the steeplechase held at Aintree each spring was the most exciting, hazardous and difficult horse race in the world. To an impressionable six-year-old the names POETHLYN, MASTER ROBERT, TIPPERARY TIM, GOLDEN MILLER and BATTLESHIP raced like magic through an imagination astonishingly brought alive. I yearned desperately to learn more about this mystical chase which could apparently create unforgettable heroes of men and horses.

When the war came to an end, the National was restored and true to his word, my dad took me to see that race in 1946, on a day when seemingly everyone had an interest in a horse called PRINCE REGENT. Sitting on my father's shoulders, we were among over 300,000 spectators and from our position on the rails at Becher's Brook, the experience was completely exhilarating. So much so, I knew I had to learn everything possible about this incredible steeplechase and without realising it, the effort to do so required greater attention to academic studies.

Learning to read was the first step to understanding the mysteries of the National, quickly followed by a greater appreciation of history, for so much of the race traces the relatively recent story of domestic and international activities. Arithmetic was never a strong point of mine but even that became, in some inexplicable way, understandable through the intricacies of the betting world, enabling me to understand the meaning of starting prices like 11/4, 15/2 and 100/6.

For my twelfth birthday I received the most wonderful gift, a book by Con O'Leary entitled *Grand National* and that most difficult task of learning to read was so richly rewarded. Like many of his countrymen before and since, Irish-born O'Leary had a very special literary gift, that rare ability to capture the reader from the opening page until with reluctance one reached The End. A true wordsmith of the highest calibre, he wove a magical spell through every line of that gem of a book, which still remains one of my fondest possessions. Subsequently the works of such fine authors as Finch Mason, David Hoadley Munroe, the American Paul Brown and the inimitable Clive Graham, provided increased pleasure and insight into the romance of the Grand National; yet after more than half a century, my quest to absorb everything remotely associated with this greatest of all sporting occasions continues.

Since my first action-filled taste of Aintree that day when LOVELY COTTAGE outstayed the brave PRINCE REGENT, I have witnessed in the flesh every nerve-tingling National moment, experienced every varied sensation the event generates and been privileged to admire the mastery of a multitude of champions who stake everything on providing a new page for sporting history.

Right: Grand National morning in 1996 with the author and the legendary Dick Francis reminiscing about the DEVON LOCH incident which occurred exactly 40 years before

Below: The favourite and top weight PRINCE REGENT leads over the last in the 1946 National, the first to be run since the end of the Second World War. Although giving a very brave performance, PRINCE REGENT was passed in the final 400 yards by the winner LOVELY COTTAGE and runner-up JACK FINLEY

The glorious triumphant moments of CORBIERE, ALDANITI, RED RUM, SUNDEW, RUSSIAN HERO and an endless line-up of unforgettable others, remain always in what Con O'Leary describes as 'the twilight of memory'. So many gallant, if heartbreaking, efforts by such as DURHAM EDITION, MR SNUGFIT, SPARTAN MISSILE, WYNDBURGH, TUDOR LINE and MACMOFFAT, must surely be recalled whenever reflections on the National are mulled over.

For me, there have also been moments of anguish and anger, such as when apathy and ineptitude threatened the very existence of the race for too many years and again, sadly, in 1993 when the race had to be declared void. Serious lessons were well learned, however, and in 1997 one could rejoice that terrorism had been overcome, through the prompt action of Aintree's management and the magnificent response of the local people in caring for and comforting many thousands of stranded racegoers.

There can be no possible way I can claim to have seen all that the Grand National has to offer, since each year's race continues to confound and intrigue. Also, my own 'race' – like that of the leaders in the National – must surely be nearing the point at which the Melling Road is crossed for the final time and all that is left is that long slog home to uncertainty.

I can say, though, that for me the Grand National stands supreme as an example of true sportsmanship in its purest form and that we can all be immensely proud of those who demonstrate such determination and commitment in making it so.

One final hope in closing: maybe one day some youngster will find between the covers of this book the inspiration and satisfaction I inherited from two genuine lovers of the horse, John Green and Con O'Leary.

Reg Green

WEIGHING ROOM &
UNSADDLING ENCLOSURE

GRAND NATIONAL

HISTORICAL BACKGROUND

1

GRAND® NATIONAL

— AINTREE —

MOST APPROPRIATELY, it is to Ireland – 'The Land Where the Horse is King' – that we must go to find the first recorded document referring to the pastime soon to be known as steeplechasing. For many years 'pounding matches' had been held by local gentry in various counties of the emerald Isle, but not until 1752 was one such match actually registered. According to this written account, a Mr O'Calloghan and his friend, Edmund Blake, struck a bet to race each other on their horses across country from Buttevant Church to the steeple of St Leger Church. From this casual match over roughly four and half miles, the sport of 'steeple-chasing' came into being.

Left: The first ever running of the Grand National. Having deposited Captain Becher in the Brook, his mount CONRAD can be seen on the far side of the tree facing the wrong way.

Although these early contests were slow affairs, they were undoubtedly arduous and potentially quite dangerous, for no competitor could know what lay behind a hedge, fence or stone wall. Not for many years would attempts be made to regulate the line of country raced over or introduce any stringent rules to the proceedings; for most involved, the whole practice was conducted in a rather slap-happy manner.

Towards the end of the eighteenth century, the nearest equivalent to Irish cross-country racing began in England in the form of fox hunting. Those participating soon realised that for this activity lighter and faster horses were required. As a result, thoroughbred stallions began being used to breed hunters and in due course this led to tremendous rivalry among owners, particularly in counties with good galloping land such as Leicestershire.

At the time of the Napoleonic wars cavalry officers became interested in competing in cross-country events and in 1804 the first military steeplechase took place near Newcastle-upon-Tyne between two Captains, Tucker and Prescott, of the 5th Light Dragoons. Around the same period three riders took part in an eight mile event wearing owner's colours for the first time, and in 1810 the first purpose built course was built in Bedford.

In 1815, the year of Waterloo, jump racing's first entrepreneur Tom Coleman set up as a trainer near Brocket Hall in Hertfordshire and such was his success, he took charge of horses belonging to such dignitaries as Lord Palmerston and Lord Melbourne. As he prospered so he diversified his interests to include that of inn-keeper, purchasing the Chequers Tavern in St Albans, which he

proceeded to pull down and replace with extensive stable accommodation and a new hostelry called the Turf Hotel. A favourite watering hole for cavalry officers and leading racing personalities, it was here that the first suggestion of a grand local steeplechase came from some members of the Life Guards. The outcome was the Great St Albans Steeplechase, run for the first time in 1830. Benefiting from Tom Coleman's outstanding organisational talents, it proved to be a total success.

The race produced the largest number of runners yet seen in a cross-country race, sixteen in all, and it was the first time in which flags were used in such an event. With the practice being to keep the route of the contest secret, Coleman used flag men concealed in ditches whose duty was to raise their flags only when the start of the race was signalled. With many contestants getting lost on the journey, Lord Ranelagh's grey horse WONDER won from the only other finisher NAILER.

Such was the favourable publicity attached to each St Albans Steeplechase, by 1834 many others were imitating Coleman's enterprise at various locations throughout the country and it was in this year a jockey named Jem Mason was seen for the first time on a racecourse when partnering THE POET in the race. Despite his mount refusing at the first fence, Mason persevered with THE POET to score a shock victory and five years later at a place called Aintree the jockey was to write his own special chapter into racing history.

Tom Coleman's involvement with the sport extended beyond organising races into that of ownership and in this he was equally successful, due in no small measure to having one of the great cross-country riders – Captain Martin Becher – to partner his horses. Becher won the St Albans Steeplechase in 1835 on a horse called NORMA, despite his mount falling during the race and he having to remount. One can well imagine from the victories of Jem Mason and Captain Becher, these early chases were run at a far slower pace than is the case today.

Although by now racing across country had became a popular spectator sport, with new races being introduced all over the country, Tom Coleman's template for the activity began to fall into decline and in 1836 just five horses competed for the prize. Becoming discouraged and also concerned that a disreputable element were now associating themselves with the sport in a most unscrupulous manner, Coleman seriously considered relinquishing his involvement and it was only the insistence of Austrian diplomat Prince Paul Esterhazy that persuaded him to continue. The Prince

generously put up a Gold Cup towards the prize for the event and with his usual marketing expertise Tom Coleman somehow induced sixteen owners to run their horses in the race. In a thrilling finish SPLENDOUR won by half a length from the Captain Becher-ridden SPICEY, with CINDERELLA a close up third.

In 1838 a rising star of the jumping world called LOTTERY finished third in the St Albans race and after the disqualification of first past the post MIDNIGHT, secured second place money.

Despite Tom Coleman's vigorous efforts to sustain an interest in his flagging steeplechase, the passage of time was most certainly against him as also where other race promoters, who succeeded in acquiring subscriptions for their events which made them more financially valuable contests than the St Albans race. Since his initial endeavour in 1830, the number of jump meetings had increased from three to 39 by 1838, bringing the realisation to Coleman that he was fighting a losing battle.

WHERE THE DREAM
of
'THE GREAT CHASE'
WAS BORN

LIVERPOOL 1837

The introduction of the Cheltenham Annual Grand Steeplechase in 1834, soon followed by that of the Vale of Aylesbury Chase shortly after, further increased his fears. With the latter event, run over a four mile course from Waddesdon windmill to Aylesbury church, carrying a cup valued at £50 in addition to a sweepstake of 20 guineas from each competitor, such contests quickly overtook the St Albans race in popularity and became the pattern for all other race promoters.

Tom Coleman's swansong came on New Year's Eve 1839 when he staged his last ever Great St Albans Chase with only five runners taking part. The race was won by the amateur rider William McDonough on VANDYKE. It was a sad conclusion to the man's entrepreneurial career, yet he passed into history as the 'Father of Steeplechasing', the man who paved the way for racing thrills and glory hitherto undreamt of.

Fortunately Coleman's close friend, Captain Becher, had some years before inadvertently ensured that the crusade begun by the host of the Turf Hotel would continue under the auspices of another inn-keeper based in the north west of the country.

William Lynn of the Waterloo Hotel in Liverpool's Ranelagh Street began organising flat-racing at Aintree in 1829 when he leased sufficient land from Lord Sefton and constructed a racecourse complete with a most elaborate grandstand. His first meeting at the venue took place on 7 July 1829, aided by 150 guineas from Liverpool corporation. The first race run, the Croxteth Stakes, was won by Mr Francis' MUFTI. With three fixtures a year, Lynn quickly developed the racecourse into a thriving concern and in October 1835 hurdle racing was included in his bill of fare, attracting no less a jumping personality than the famous Captain Becher. Partnering the outstanding gelding VIVIAN, on whom he had triumphed in the 1834 Vale of Aylesbury Chase, the Captain won two races within hours of each other on the bay.

Celebrating the dual victory that evening in the Waterloo Hotel, Martin Becher regaled his host with colourful tales of his friend Tom Coleman and the Great St Albans Chase to such splendid effect that Lynn began planning a steeplechase of his own for Aintree. Scarcely four months later, on 29 February 1836, William Lynn presented his first steeplechase to an enthusiastic Liverpool crowd.

Left: LOTTERY, winner of the first Grand Liverpool Steeplechase at Aintree on 26 February 1839

Far left: The famous VIVIAN with Captain Becher in the saddle. Together they won the Vale of Aylesbury Chase, the Cheltenham Steeplechase and two hurdle races on the same day at Aintree

Fittingly the race was won by the man largely responsible for its inception, Captain Becher on THE DUKE, owned locally by Mr Sirdefield, the proprietor of the George Inn at Great Crosby. Without the benefit of a title, the event also suffered somewhat slightly from a clause in the conditions of the race which presented it as a selling chase (a race which stipulates that the winning horse be put up for sale). Nevertheless, the contest over two circuits of the course and including 42 obstacles in all, was a great success and hugely appreciated by all in attendance.

Still rather cautious concerning the attitude of the sport's governing body towards cross-country racing, William Lynn conspired with fellow racecourse administrator John Formby to stage the following year's event at his course in Maghull, some three miles from Aintree. Disappointingly, only four runners competed for this 1837 event, which now bore the name the Grand Liverpool Steeplechase. It carried 100 sovereigns, donated by the town of Liverpool, and once more THE DUKE proved superior though this time without the illustrious Captain Becher in the saddle.

Yet again twelve months later the big Merseyside race was held at Maghull, this time won by SIR HENRY ridden by Tom Olliver, a man who much would subsequently be heard of in the world of steeplechasing. But William Lynn had already come to a decision: satisfied that the event had won public approval, he set about organising the 1839 steeplechase, which he planned for Aintree.

Bravely battling against ill-health, Lynn worked ceaselessly to put on a jumping showpiece to thrill and delight and one which would be remembered for years ahead. He was not alone in his optimism, for aware of the organiser's indisposition a syndicate was formed to safeguard

the interests of the event, whose race committee included the Earls of Derby, Sefton, Eglinton and Wilton, Lords George Bentinck, Stanley and Robert Grosvenor; Sirs John Gerard, Thomas Massey Stanley and RW Bulkeley.

This impressive array of enthusiasts prepared to invest money in the venture and provided great confidence in the Aintree Grand Liverpool Steeplechase, which like its forerunners received a donation towards the prize-money of 100 sovereigns from the Aldermen of Liverpool. From an original entry of 53, seventeen actually went to post on the day of the race, 26 February 1839, and an estimated 40,000 people made their way

Left: Jem Mason, the foremost jump jockey of his day, partnered LOTTERY to victory in the Grand Liverpool Chase, the Cheltenham Steeplechase twice and the Leamington Grand Annual. He married the owner's daughter, Miss Elmore, and because of his always immaculate appearance was known as 'Dandy Jem'

Left: Galway-born Alan McDonough was one of the first Irish jockeys to make a name for himself racing in England. Winning almost every important steeplechase except that at Aintree, he did however finish twice second in the Grand Liverpool

Far left: Preparing for the start of the 1839 Grand Liverpool Steeplechase. LOTTERY, the eventual winner, is in full profile on the right. On the extreme left can be seen the Earl of Sefton with William Lynn next to him on the grey

Left: Another famous Irish horseman and a benefactor to his countrymen during the potato famine, the third Marquis of Waterford came fourth on his horse THE SEA in the 1840 Grand Liverpool

by various means of transport to witness the highly publicised event.

Favourite at 5/1 was the brilliant LOTTERY, owned by John Elmore and ridden by the most acclaimed professional jockey of the age, Jem Mason. Captain Martin Becher took the mount on a horse called CONRAD who, unlike his rider, was something of an unknown quantity. The Irish were well represented with Tom Ferguson owning three of the runners and riding his most fancied, DAXON, while others attracting punters' attention included THE NUN, CHARITY and RUST.

Although the race was due to start at one o'clock, some confusion in the weighing out procedure and a succession of false starts caused such a delay that it was not until three o'clock that the field were sent on their way. Almost directly from the off, Captain Becher blazed a trail out into the country with CONRAD setting a merry gallop that a number of his opponents had trouble keeping pace with. Crossing the ploughed field on the approach to the first of the three brooks, they were many lengths clear. But, hampered by the ground, CONRAD misjudged his take-off, struck the top palings and deposited Becher into the brook. Sheltering in the water until the rest of the runners were clear, the Captain clambered out and is reported to have exclaimed, 'How dreadful water tastes without the benefit of whisky'.

He did manage to catch CONRAD and remount, only to fall at the second brook.

In the meantime, DAXON had assumed command and striding out well led LOTTERY, RUST, THE DICTATOR, CHARITY and THE NUN back towards the grandstand. CHARITY, reputedly the finest wall jumper in Gloucestershire, moved into a challenging position coming towards the end of the first circuit, but uncharacteristically refused at the Wall in front of the stands. Making a forward move going to the brook which had claimed

Becher on the first circuit, Jem Mason took LOTTERY smoothly into the lead, and staying on extremely well over the remaining obstacles, passed the winning post a very worthy winner by three lengths from Tom Olliver on SEVENTY FOUR, with the mare PAULINA third of the seven to finish.

Despite the occasion having been a tremendous success in the eyes of the majority who witnessed it, the *Liverpool Mercury* reported the following day in a rather scathing manner: 'We have heard with alarm and regret that it is in contemplation to establish steeplechasing annually or periodically in this neighbourhood. If any such design is seriously entertained we trust that some means will be adopted to defeat it'.

In what one could be forgiven for describing as a distinct change of heart, the same newspaper made the following announcement the very next week: 'We learn that upward of 50 gentlemen have subscribed to another steeplechase next year, that 40 subscriptions are fully expected and that it is anticipated the chase will be one of the most splendid ever witnessed whether as regards the patronage it will receive or the number of horses that will be entered'.

William Lynn, having created an event which was to live through and beyond the reigns of six British monarchs, bowed out gracefully an exhausted and rather melancholy man, and although he performed a minor official role at Aintree for many years, he died in 1870 virtually penniless. Speaking later in his life

Above: Jem Mason rides LOTTERY to a comfortable victory from SEVENTY FOUR, PAULINA, TRUE BLUE and Alan McDonough on THE NUN

Left: The third brook second time round with DICTATOR coming to grief, leaving LOTTERY and SEVENTY FOUR in the lead

about his Aintree activities, Lynn dejectedly made the following observation: 'It has been a most unlucky speculation for me. I should have been worth at least £30,000 if I had never had anything to do with it. Now I have to begin the world all over again after 30 years industry'.

The Grand Liverpool Steeplechase had also seen the last of Captain Becher, who although continuing to ride across country until 1847, never rode in the race again. His name, however, lives on and is remembered each spring when the National runners face up to the awesome Brook which bears his name.

The Jockey Club's continuing animosity towards steeplechasing did little to deter the the widespread appeal of the sport, with more meetings cropping up all over the place. With the Grand National by now far and away the general public's favourite horse race, many racecourse administrators sought to invent a contest to rival its popularity. In 1867 the Scottish Grand National was inaugurated at Bogside, followed three years later by the introduction at Fairyhouse of the Irish equivalent. For cross-country enthusiasts within the armed forces, the Grand Military meeting came into being also in 1867.

So famous had the Aintree National by now become, though, it alone continued to be the supreme test for horse and rider, the one race everyone wanted to win and very much the most thrilling race for spectators in the calendar. To regulate steeplechasing's affairs and control the behaviour of those involved in the sport, the National Hunt Committee was founded in 1866 thanks largely to the efforts of Mr 'Cherry' Angell, Mr Craven and Lord Grey de Wilton, and assisted by a devoted assembly of chasing enthusiasts they worked ceaselessly to inspire confidence in

the sport. For Benjamin John Angell it was the culmination of many years of strenuous effort to improve the image of steeplechasing and less than twelve months before achieving his goal he received a premature reward when winning the Grand National with the five-year-old chestnut ALCIBIADE.

An encouraging aspect of the newly formed authority was that the majority of the fourteen founder members already served as members of the Jockey Club, although most of those associated with flat racing's governing body still preferred to keep a 'respectable' distance between themselves and the affairs of steeplechasing.

Introducing new and enforceable rules for chasing was the first and most important function of the National Hunt Committee. By the end of 1866, among ample entries in their Minute Book, appeared the following entry: 'The decision of the Stewards, or whomsoever they may appoint, is final in everything connected with steeplechases, and there is no apppeal whatever to a court of law'.

Severe criticism of the sport was to remain for some time yet, however, from a variety of sources and quite often in extremely vitriolic terms. For example, there was the document produced by Lord William Lennox which expressed these observations: 'Steeplechasing is very popular in February, but we own that it is with regret that we find this break-neck pursuit so much in the ascendancy, for to our ideas it cannot come under the denomination of legitimate sport. If, during, or at the end of a hunting season, gentlemen like to try the merits of their respective horses over four or five miles of a fair country, there can be no possible objection to such a proceeding - on the contrary it is an amusing and harmless recreation. But when horses that have never followed a hound, ridden by professional jockeys, are brought out to gallop three or four miles over a racecourse with stiff stone walls, strong post and rails, awfully large artificial brooks, hurdles, thick fences and broad ditches, the whole feature is destroyed. Instead of its being a test of the goodness of a hunter, it degenerates to a mere gambling racing transaction, in which the best horse seldom ever or never wins, for with a field of fifteen or sixteen, the chances are that the

favourites are put *hors de combat* by the rush and pressing of the others'.

With those for and against steeplechasing entrenched in their own particular opinions, controversy was set to continue for many years to come, yet Mr Angell and his associates strove with determination to improve the reputation of the sport they served so well. After an onslaught of disapproval from various sources, an article in *Bell's Life* provided some much needed reassurance for the National Hunt Committee, while at the same time unwittingly providing an answer to the problem of overall acceptance for chasing. Strangely prophetic, this feature read as follows: 'Truly gratifying to the lovers of steeplechasing is the present state and prospects of that all invigorating and glorious

Above: Captain Henry Coventry of the Grenadier Guards won the National at his first attempt in 1865 aboard ALCIBIADE but never competed in the race again. He was a cousin of Lord Coventry who owned both EMBLEM and EMBLEMATIC to win the race in 1863 and 1864

Left: ALCIBIADE won the honours in 1865 for his owner Benjamin John Angell, whose initiative and dedication led to the founding of a governing body for the sport, The National Hunt Committee, twelve months later

sport. Whilst, however, consistently exposing its abuses we have ever steadily upheld steeplechasing as a national sport and vindicated it as a pursuit calculated alike to test the mettle and merits of the horse and his rider. In the good work of endeavouring to bring about a better state of things, we were ably supported by a few "good men and true", and the result is a triumphant and gratifying one. With laws to protect it, countenanced by Royalty and patronised by the leading sportsmen of the day, steeplechasing is no longer the "illegitimate" despised thing it was, but now ranks proudly side by side with other ennobling and manly pastimes'.

Strengthening their position of control of all events involving steeplechases and hurdle races, the National Hunt Committee slowly but surely reorganised, improved and stimulated everyone and everything associated with the sport. Although some skulduggery was to continue for many years, all offenders were sought out and severely dealt with, gradually creating the confidence the sport so desperately

needed. As predicted in the *Bell's Life* article, National Hunt racing did indeed eventually receive Royal patronage, from none other than Albert Edward Prince of Wales, who encouraged by his close friend and fellow sportsman Lord Marcus Beresford, became an owner of jumpers in addition to his many flat race horses.

His Royal Highness became extremely knowledgeable in both the bloodstock industry and the affairs of the Turf, enjoying much success with his flat horses and subsequently also with his jumpers. In the mid-1870s CHIMNEY SWEEP, owned by Lord Marcus Beresford, was placed three times in the Grand National and from then on the Prince of Wales was determined to have a runner in the race. His first involvement in the National came in 1879 as part owner, with his friend Lord Marcus, of the eleven-year-old JACKAL which finished second behind THE LIBERATOR. Five years later in 1884, the heir apparent to the British throne was the named owner of THE SCOT, a son of a former Derby winner that started 6/1 National favourite and after jumping

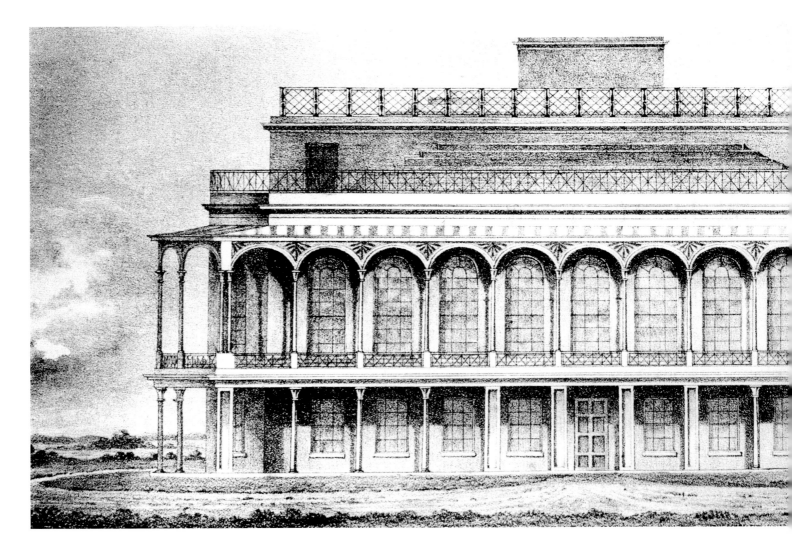

splendidly for most of the journey fell at the second Canal Turn. For most of the next 25 years the Prince of Wales had a runner in the Grand National and his Aintree reward for such valuable support did eventually materialise, as will be seen later.

The importance of the involvement in steeplechasing by the British Royal Family cannot be over-emphasised, for it brought with it the aura of respectability so essential to the sport and its future. From that time on National Hunt racing flourished, with new valuable and prestigious events being added to the fixture list on a regular basis. Possibly the most important of these, the Whitbread Gold Cup, presented an exciting initiative, for the three mile five furlong steeplechase introduced at Sandown Park in 1957 was the first to carry substantial sponsorship. Through their generous

Left: The Fourth Earl of Sefton, whose family leased the racecourse at Aintree for racing and agricultural purposes until Mrs Topham purchased it from them in 1949

financial backing, brewers Whitbread set a trend which within a few short years totally revitalised National Hunt racing. With other commercial entities following their example, the traditional 'poor relation of flat racing' suddenly received an unexpected and much needed financial shot in the arm.

As the centenary of the founding of the National Hunt Committee approached, the fine contribution it had made to the advance and prosperity of 'racing over the sticks' was recognised. In 1963 it became part of a joint authority entitled the Turf Board, set up by the Senior Steward of the Jockey Club and consisting of Stewards from both assemblies. The exercise proved such a success that in 1969 the Jockey Club and the National Hunt Committee formed an amalgamation, the activities of which now come under the jurisdiction of the recently formed British Horseracing Board.

Pre-eminent today of all meetings under National Hunt rules is the Cheltenham Festival held each March, featuring the Champion Hurdle Challenge Cup and the Cheltenham Gold Cup, both introduced during the 1920s and, of course, that important link with the early years of jump racing, the Cheltenham Grand Annual Steeplechase.

Left: Aintree's first grandstand, known as the 'Wedding Cake stand', was designed by Liverpool architect John Foster junior and accidentally destroyed by fire in 1892

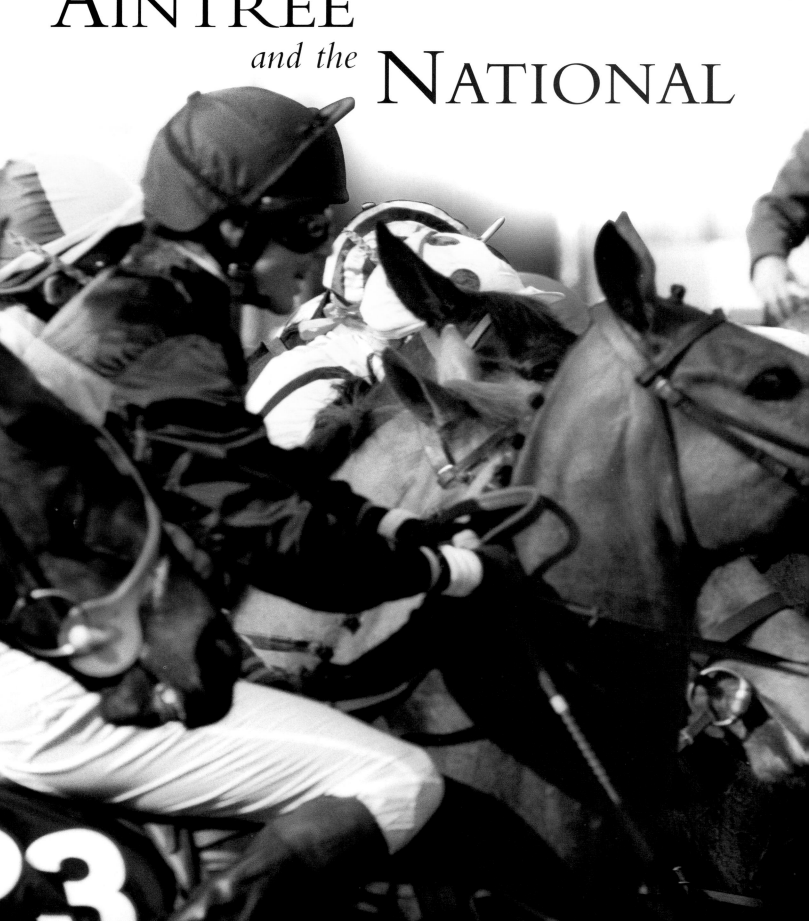

AINTREE
and the NATIONAL

2

GRAND® NATIONAL
— AINTREE —

EVEN FOR THOSE NOT INTERESTED in horse racing, Aintree means only one thing: the greatest, most demanding and thrilling steeplechase ever devised.

The word is, in fact, a derivative of the Anglo Saxon 'an-treow' meaning 'One Tree', with early records often converting the form to 'Ayntre' or 'Ayntree', but certainly it is as Aintree that the village some seven miles from the centre of Liverpool has achieved worldwide fame as the home of the Grand National. Incorporated with Liverpool in 1905, it was already by then the annual scene of a mass influx of many thousands of people from every corner of the world.

Left: The atmosphere is always tense as the jockeys await the starter's instructions

It is thanks to Liverpool inn-keeper William Lynn that we are annually treated to racing's finest spectacle, for he it was who dreamed of an event to rival that of Tom Coleman's Great St Albans Steeplechase, ironically influenced by Coleman's close friend Captain Becher. Having administered Aintree's flat racing since first leasing the racecourse in 1829, and with the new sport of cross-country racing frowned on by most of the nobility, it was a brave enterprise Lynn embarked upon. So had been his venture with the Waterloo Cup hare coursing event at nearby Altcar, yet that had proved successful.

Originally the inn-keeper's only claim to fame had been his renown as 'The Finest Fryer of Fish in the Kingdom'. Though always with his eye to business in a Liverpool at the height of its commercial potential, his involvement in promoting sporting events naturally took precedence. After much soul-searching regarding the wisdom of his involvement with an activity held in contempt by the Jockey Club, William Lynn threw himself whole-heartedly into presenting an event he felt certain would 'enthrall, delight and excite all who witnessed it'.

It is most interesting to inspect the conditions for Aintree's first Grand Liverpool Steeplechase, held on Tuesday, 26 February 1839, which contained the following stipulations: 'A sweepstake of twenty sovereigns each, five sovereigns forfeit, with one hundred sovereigns added; twelve stone each; gentleman riders; four miles across country; the second horse to save his stake, and the winner to pay ten sovereigns towards expenses; no rider to open a gate or ride

Right: LITTLE CHARLEY, winner of the Grand National in 1858 when ridden by William Archer, father of the legendary flat race champion jockey

Far right: Mrs Mirabel Dorothy Topham, who took control of Aintree when her husband Ronald suffered ill health. Through her dynamism and intuition she restored the racecourse after the Second World War, purchased it from Lord Sefton in 1949 and built both the Mildmay chase course and Grand Prix motor race track

through a gateway; or more than one hundred yards along any road, footpath or driftway'.

Contrary to this, the actual distance was a little more than four miles and even more significantly only five of the seventeen competing riders could justly claim to be 'gentlemen riders', or as we know them today, true amateurs. As has already been well documented, LOTTERY won that first contest and having laid the foundations of an event which achieved even more than its promoter could ever have contemplated, that man who first won acclaim as a fish fryer gracefully faded from the scene.

That Edward William Topham was chosen to handicap the race in 1843 was a decision based, not merely on the man's unique expertise in such a role, but more importantly on the fact that he was totally and obviously dedicated to the future prosperity of Aintree racecourse. Through him alone came innovations years ahead of their time and a commitment which was to endure through 125 years of his family's association with Liverpool's racecourse. That first big Aintree handicap, named the Liverpool and National Steeplechase, was the foundation of a dynasty which brought the race from the tenuous uncertainty of the nineteenth century to the final third of the twentieth with a reputation admired by all.

Although the Grand National would always remain the highlight of events at Aintree, the purpose for which the racecourse was originally established – flat racing – remained its principal function and would continue to do so for many years to come. During the nineteenth century such celebrated exponents of flat race jockeyship as Sam Loates, George Fordham, Tom Cannon and the greatest of all, Fred Archer, regularly added to their winning tally through visits to Aintree. Sad to relate, it was the gift of a pistol presented by Liverpool Racecourse to the brilliant though tragic Fred Archer which became the instrument of his death. After winning the Liverpool St Leger on THEBAIS in 1884, the jockey's young wife Nellie died giving birth to a daughter just days later. Almost two years to the day after his sad loss, in a fit of depression after recovering from a severe illness, heartbroken Fred Archer shot himself with the silver firearm given to him at Aintree. He was only 29 years of age at the time. It is a strange coincidence that at Aintree in November 1933, the then hero of flat racing Gordon Richards equalled the record of 246 winners in a season set up by Fred Archer in 1885, before proceeding to surpass it by 13 before the end of the year.

Shortly after the Second World War, 'The Boy Wonder Jockey' Lester Keith Piggott became the third generation of his family to ride at Aintree, his first triumph at the venue being on LITTLE BONNET in a flat race on 9 November 1949, just four days after his fourteenth birthday. Lester Piggott was to partner many winners at Liverpool during his incredibly

successful career, including four at the July fixture in 1958, two of which were trained by Bill Dutton who rode TIPPERARY TIM to win the calamitous Grand National of 1928. On the first day of the 1967 National meeting, Lester scored an Aintree flat race double with MISS PESETA and MAJOR ROSE and just 24 hours later an equine racing legend made his racecourse debut in a five furlong selling plate for two-year-olds. Sharing half the prize-money in that contest by dead-heating, RED RUM had made an unlikely start to a racing occupation which was to spread his name around the world. Of the ten races on the flat contested by RED RUM, he was partnered in two by Lester Piggott. Under top weight of eight stone five pounds he finished third under the champion jockey in the Minor Nursery Handicap at Pontefract and the following year, roughly an hour after RED ALLIGATOR won the 1968 National, was beaten by a short-head by ALAN'S PET in the Earl of Sefton's Plate at Aintree.

By this time the future of Liverpool racecourse and the Grand National was seriously in the balance, with each year's race dubbed by the media as the last.

Mrs Mirabel Dorothy Topham had succeeded her husband Ronald as head of Tophams Limited when that gentleman suffered a serious illness, and she purchased the racecourse from its owner Lord Sefton in 1949 for a sum said to be in the region of £250,000. With no Levy Board in existence at the time to assist her financial requirements, Mrs

Topham began the 1950s with an ambitious building programme, which included the construction of both the Mildmay Steeplechase course on the stands side of Melling Road and also that of a Grand Prix motor race circuit following the route of the National itself.

In addition to many other auto-sport activities, Aintree hosted a number of Grand Prix events, both British and European championship races, and among the successful drivers were such household names as Mike Hawthorn, Stirling Moss and Juan Fangio. By

Above: Motor racing ace Stirling Moss being presented with the victor's laurel wreath after winning a Grand Prix at Aintree in the 1950s

the middle of the 1960s, however, falling attendances and shortage of funds made it impossible for Mrs Topham to continue and she reluctantly decided to find a buyer for Aintree. Eventually reduced to just one fixture a year – the spring Grand National meeting - Aintree and its historic steeplechase became a forlorn shadow of its former glory; the stands falling into disrepair, facilities for racegoers meagre and that ominous question mark perpetually hanging over a perilously uncertain future.

In October 1972 a glimmer of hope appeared when, through the sponsorship of bookmakers William Hill Limited, the old Grand Sefton meeting was restored, albeit as a single day's fixture. A mixed card of flat, hurdle and steeplechase races brought huge crowds back to the racecourse, with the principal event the William Hill Grand National Trial over two miles and seven furlongs of the Grand National course.

Finally, in December 1973, Mrs Topham sold Aintree racecourse to the Liverpool-born property developer Mr Bill Davies for £3 million, ending a family association with the Grand National which began with the 'Wizard', Edward William Topham, way back in 1843.

Whatever the original intention of Mr Davies, his plans took something of a nosedive when first he failed to obtain planning permission for certain parts of the racecourse

Right: Aintree's new owner Bill Davies with Mrs Topham after purchasing the racecourse in December 1973

and then, more seriously, when the bottom appeared to fall out of the property market. To the general public it seemed as if little headway had been made through the sale of the racecourse and, in 1975, when admission charges were increased three-fold, the smallest attendance for a Grand National in living memory announced its displeasure.

Yet again the irritating suspicion that the Grand National had lost its attraction to not only much of the general public but to the racing authorities as well, once more placed the event in a precarious position. Himself now seeking a buyer for the apparently doomed racecourse, Bill Davies finally entered into an agreement with Mr Cyril Stein, the head of Ladbrokes, in which the bookmaking firm would manage and administrate Aintree for the next seven years. At a time of despondency, it was refreshing to discover that at least the betting industry realised some potential within the world's greatest steeplechase, and as the 1976 Grand National drew near it became obvious that Ladbrokes' involvement was well designed.

The whole of their marketing, public relations and advertising machine moved promptly into action, working strenuously to complete a preparation worthy of an event of such international acclaim. Ladbrokes' impact on Aintree was immediate and thorough, with newly appointed Clerk of the Course John Hughes displaying unique qualities of leadership, together with an assortment of innovative concepts which impressed all attending the 1976 National. A comforting sense of well-being reassured everyone that the ills of the past could be cured under this new regime and although still owned by the troubled Bill Davies, Aintree at last seemed to have been handed a lifeline.

With efficiency and determination, Ladbrokes' temporary management of Liverpool racecourse inspired new hope among the public, with attendances each spring rising to encouraging levels.

Such unforgettable performances as that of RED RUM winning his third National in 1977 and Bob Champion with ALDANITI capturing the hearts of all in that emotion-filled 1981 race, endorsed the view that the Grand

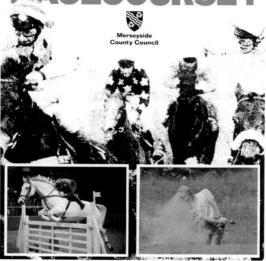

The future of AINTREE RACECOURSE?

Merseyside County Council

National was too valuable a part of Britain's sporting heritage to allow it to wither and die. Yet by the time the Ladbrokes contract expired in 1982, the sale of Aintree remained unresolved and at the request of the Jockey Club, the bookmaking firm performed one final administrative duty in organising the 1983

Below: DELMOSS leads the eventual winner CORBIERE over the Chair in 1983. DELMOSS finished tenth and was subsequently auctioned, with the proceeds going to the Appeal Committee set up to save the National

event. The result was another record-breaking occasion, with CORBIERE providing Jenny Pitman with a memorable victory in becoming the first woman to train a winner of the race.

Still, incredibly, the future of the world's most famous steeplechase remained dreadfully uncertain, despite a public appeal aimed at raising funds to assist the purchase of the racecourse. With plans already in place to transfer the race in name only to Doncaster, the media, general public and racing world itself shook their lowered heads in resignation and prepared to accept the inevitable fact that the Grand National was beyond saving.

Mercifully a man with first hand experience of the demands, heartbreak and very special qualities generated by the National, achieved through the written word what had eluded so many. Lord John Oaksey, who as amateur rider John Lawrence came so close to winning the 1963 National on CARRICKBEG, expressed with such incisive magnetism in a *Daily Telegraph* feature just what the Grand National stood for and how enormous a loss would be its passing, that a certain Major Ivan Straker acted promptly and decisively.

As chairman and chief executive of Seagram UK Limited, Major Straker immediately contacted Mr Bronffman, the head of the Canadian distilling company, and received permission to enter into a

sponsorship package which, virtually at the eleventh hour, saved the National.

Since HALLO DANDY won the first Seagram Grand National in 1984, the stature of the race has gone from strength to strength, an entire programme of improvements to Aintree's facilities have made it one of the best equipped racecourses in the land, and the Liverpool spring Grand National meeting now rivals the Cheltenham National Hunt Festival.

The victory of aptly named SEAGRAM in 1991 brought the curtain down on Seagram UK's sponsorship of the race, but with their subsidiary company – Martell - taking over financial responsibility for the meeting, the success of their commitment to Aintree has been equally thorough.

Martell's generous involvement with the entire three-day Grand National fixture has raised the level of prize-money on offer to record levels, attracting the finest jumpers from far and wide as competitors, and restoring the Grand National to its rightful place as a major international sporting event.

THERE
to be JUMPED

3

GRAND® NATIONAL
—AINTREE—

WITH SIXTEEN OBSTACLES, fourteen of which need to be jumped twice, the Grand National's notorious fences have woven a mystical tale of bravery, misfortune and tragedy for over 160 years. Now, as when they were first encountered, they remain the most daunting barriers to success ever faced.

Steeplechasing today is highly organised, professionally administered and considered by many a far greater spectacle than its flat-race counterpart, but there is a distinct difference between conventional chasing and racing over Aintree's Grand National fences. Every jumping course in the country, including that known as the Mildmay course at Aintree, consists of what are commonly known as 'park' fences. The difference between both forms of obstacle lies in its construction.

Left: Corbiere leaps Becher's during the 1983 National

Park fences are built with tightly packed birch, allowing a certain amount of give at the uppermost extremities, whereas those met on the National course are assembled with a base of thick branches embedded in the ground, covered by an inviting top dressing of spruce. Without the flexibility of a conventional fence, the Grand National obstacles are 'there to be jumped' in every sense of the word, for the slightest liberty taken will result in a tumbling horse and an empty saddle.

As National Hunt racing developed under diligent control by its organising committee, enclosed racecourses adhered to the rules applied to them, such as a set number of regulation sized obstacles to each mile. With Aintree, however, it was impractical to impose such principles. Accordingly the layout of the Grand National course still follows very much the route taken in the days of LOTTERY and Captain Becher, with most of the fences in approximately the same positions.

That changes have been made to the obstacles over the years, particularly in the twentieth century, came through necessity and a desire to make the race as safe as possible for both horse and rider, while retaining its unique character. One major feature of Liverpool racecourse which couldn't be altered was the contours of the land, which beyond the Melling Road create the drops on the landing side of the fences. Merely referred to as 'drop fences', they are an important link with early cross-country racing in general and the Grand Liverpool Chase in particular. Competing over a natural country as was the practice then, contestants jumped whatever barrier they met from one field into the next and invariably that meant from one level of ground to a lower one. The most pronounced drop of all was and still remains that on the landing side of the notorious Becher's Brook.

We are fortunate that somebody on that memorable day in 1839 took the trouble to describe at least some of the obstructions that pioneering group of horses and riders faced. His vague though valuable description reads: 'The first fence was a high bank with rails or, in some places, gorse on top. Other fences of a similar formidable nature included a high bank with a five foot ditch on the take-off side and deep ploughed field on the landing side. A post

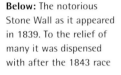

Below: The notorious Stone Wall as it appeared in 1839. To the relief of many it was dispensed with after the 1843 race

and rails in front of a fence with a six foot brook on the landing side; the take-off being out of plough. Through the mishap of CONRAD this fence was henceforth known as Becher's Brook. A high hedge, bank and rails in front of fifteen foot of water with a drop. The "Table Jump" where the landing was four foot higher than the take-off side, a most difficult fence to take at racing speed. A stone wall four foot nine inches to five foot high'.

Though Captain Becher's christening of the first Brook in 1839 is well documented, less well known is how Valentine's Brook received its name. In 1840 an Irish amateur rider named Alan Power laid a heavy bet that he and his horse VALENTINE would be first to arrive at the Wall. Intent on collecting from his gamble, he set off at a furious pace at the head of the field. Well clear approaching the third Brook, VALENTINE inexplicably slowed to almost a standstill just yards from the fence. At the very last moment the horse suddenly had a change of heart, leapt forward and with an acrobatic corkscrew-type jump, cleared the fence and Brook to race on and secure his owner's bet and eventually finish third in the race behind the winner JERRY.

Interesting to note in the aforementioned description of the racecourse, no mention was made of the hurdles which were included in the contest nor the fact that most of those described had to be jumped twice, but possibly the most important feature of this most valuable account is the reference to 'ploughed' expanses of the racecourse. An obvious component of farmland, a ploughed field was also of course an integral hazard of cross-country racing, especially when heavy rain turned it into a quagmire. Certainly in the case of Aintree, it was to be many years before the entire racing area would be completely turfed.

The practice of purposefully flagging the fences in steelechasing reached a level of supreme importance in the Grand National of 1857 when the race was run in a torrential downpour on very heavy going. Jockey Charlie Boyce rode in the race with one arm strapped to his body after injuring it in a hunting accident. Having noticed a stretch of good ground on the first circuit, he steered his mount EMIGRANT on to what was in effect the canal towpath second

time round. His three-length victory was rewarded by the owners of the horse with a present of £1,000, but the stewards were rather less than pleased, implying that Boyce had gained an unfair advantage over his rivals. From that day on, all steeplechase obstacles were required to be flagged at each end of the fence.

Contrary to its intended purpose, Aintree's Stone Wall, far from being the object of approving sightseers, aroused anger through a severity which eliminated many fine horses. Bowing to public pressure, the obstacle was finally removed in 1844, having been used just three times in the first five years of the race. Replacing it with a far less treacherous ten-foot wide Water Jump, the organisers welcomed the approval of spectators who felt pleased with the alterations.

Above: EMIGRANT, the winner in 1857, when the tactics employed by his jockey Charlie Boyce led to all the Aintree fences being flagged

Below: An unexpected and extra jump for THE LAMB as he is confronted by two fallen horses en route to a second victory

Above: The Home of the Brave! This aerial view of Aintree Racecourse gives a superb impression of the task awaiting any would-be winner of the Grand National

After the tragic death of jockey James Wynne at the fence before the Water in 1862, it was felt that with that obstacle being a plain fence which was regularly taken at great speed, it would be advisable to change it to an open ditch. In due course this rail, ditch and fence became known as The Chair, as a result of being positioned directly alongside the seat always occupied by the distance judge.

From its early prosperity, the Grand National suffered from a fall in favour by the early 1860s, mainly because the obstacles had become so small they presented hardly any challenge, and serious efforts were made by Aintree's management to address the problem. In 1885 the whole of the Grand National racecourse was fully turfed, removing the tiring stretches of open plough, and running rails were erected in the inside of the course for the entire journey. By now also, the race had moved away from being an event principally for hunter types, with many more thoroughbreds

being aimed at the National, and this led to faster times for the race being recorded by the winners. Although hunters would continue to play an important role in National Hunt racing and indeed the Grand National, more and more 'cast-offs' from flat racing were being turned to jumping and by the end of the nineteenth century Aintree's great steeplechase was not only the most prestigious event of its kind but also by far the most valuable.

One of the first American sportsmen to become actively involved in the National was Mr Foxhall Keene, whose white and blue spotted colours were twice carried in the race in the early years of the twentieth century. After 1908 when RUBIO became the first United States-bred winner of the race, many wealthy owners from across the Atlantic became captivated by the event, regularly purchasing horses simply to represent them at Aintree. Encouraged by the victories of American owned SERGEANT MURPHY and JACK HORNER in 1923 and 1926, Mr Howard Bruce sent over his brilliant Kentucky-bred BILLY BARTON to contest the 1928 Grand National. Such was the fame of the horse, the BBC's radio commentary of the race attracted a large audience of listeners back in the States.

Run on the last Friday of March 1928, the National field of 42 runners was the largest yet to compete for the coveted trophy, a fact which, coupled with the heavy state of the ground, led many to believe the race would develop into chaos. Not even the most pessimistic, though, could have envisaged just what the outcome was to be. Only the 100/1 outsider TIPPERARY TIM survived the course without mishap, after his sole remaining rival BILLY BARTON fell at the final fence when appearing to have the race in his pocket. With jockey Tommy Cullinan remounting BILLY BARTON to finish a remote second, they were the only others to collect a share of the prize-money.

The cause of the catastrophe was the front-running EASTER HERO toppling into the open ditch at the Canal Turn on the first circuit, trotting backwards and forwards along its length and bringing all but a handful of those following to a standstill. After an immediate inquiry the racecourse management decided to fill in the ditch and since then the Canal Turn obstacle has been a plain fence, whilst of course still keeping its notorious 90 degree left-hand turn.

For the second time in its history, the National faced interruption by a world war in 1939 and after BOGSKAR won the wartime race of 1940, the racecourse was again handed over for the use of the War Department. With peace restored, Tophams Limited faced a monumental task in restoring the racecourse to a condition capable of hosting the renewal of the great race in 1946, but under the supervision of Mrs Topham the race was run before 300,000 war-weary though jubilant spectators. With the winner LOVELY COTTAGE being ridden to victory by a Captain Bobby Petre, who was on demob leave from the Scots Guards, the first post-war National carried on the tradition of annual fairy tales.

Always and still the most demanding steeplechase of all, the Grand National has

Below: A revamped Canal Turn for the 1929 National with the ditch a thing of the past and the obstacle now a plain fence

Above: Measuring the ditch at The Chair in preparation for a 1930s race

Right: Foot-perfect at Becher's Brook first time round in 1933

never been far from controversy of one kind or another, and during the 1950s came in for criticism of such vehemence that questions were asked in Parliament concerning the race's severity and alleged unfairness to horses. Bombarded with calls for either the complete banning of the race or major alterations to the fences, Mrs Topham relented and after MERRYMAN II romped home in 1960, began a programme of modification to all the obstacles on the National course. The former completely upright fences were given a pronounced slope on the take-off side, away from the runners, permitting them to be taken at an angle of 50 degrees instead of the previous 65 degrees. In addition, the fender at the base of the fences was increased to allow horses and riders an improved view of their line of approach, and dispensing with gorse as a means of dressing some of the fences was a most welcome improvement.

Full credit must be given to Mrs Topham for implementing these changes, which involved a good deal of effort and finance, at a time when only seven races per year were conducted over the National course.

Welcoming the observations of the Royal Society for the Prevention of Cruelty to Animals, Tophams Limited worked closely with the organisation for many years in their efforts to improve safety at Aintree and the

same amicable relationship exists with the present racecourse management. But as with any other physical pastime or activity, accidents do happen in spite of every effort being made to avoid them. Nobody feels grief more deeply through an injury to a horse than those most closely involved in the care and welfare of the animal.

Emergency facilities are essential at all racecourses and at Aintree no less than eight veterinary surgeons are in attendance to administer treatment to any horse needing it,

Above: Inspector of racecourses Gilbert Cotton with Aintree's Clerk of the Course Jim Bidwell-Topham examining the track before the race

Below: The awesome Taxis fence in the Czech Republic's *Velka Pardubice* Steeplechase, a race often compared with Aintree's event in terms of severity

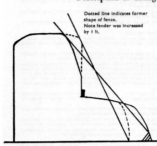

GRAND NATIONAL STEEPLE CHASE

Description of Changes made to the Fences and Conditions in 1961

Dotted line indicates former shape of fence.
Note fender was increased by 1 ft.

An improved approach to the great Aintree Fences was made which now enforces a jump being taken at an angle of 50 degrees instead of 65 degrees, as so often happened in the rapid speed at which the race is run.

It was also decided to reduce the top weight from 12 st. 7 lb. to 12 st. and to place a three year time limit on qualification.

In 1958 the Directors of the Irish Hospitals Sweepstakes wishing to pay tribute to this supreme test of Horse and Rider, of which they hear much from 147 Countries, decided to support the famous 'Chase with a generous donation of £5,000 towards the Prize Money, which support they have since continued.

Although this kept the Stakes of the Grand National Steeple Chase well ahead of all other Chases, sponsored racing was growing. The Executive feeling that Honour and Glory might play second fiddle to the commercial instinct, made an appeal on this point which was fortunately heard by someone counting merit first.

In consequence, in 1961 the well-known, old-established Firm of Messrs. Schweppes Limited sportingly agreed to donate £7,500 to The Grand National Steeple chase, being £5,000 to the race and £2,500 to special prizes to Trainers, Riders and Stables, adopting as a slogan—" Schweppes and the Grand National in a class by themselves ".

This greatly increased the International interest in the race, drawing not only a French Entry but three Russian ones which greatly appealed to the Public.

THE 1961 GRAND NATIONAL STEEPLE CHASE CONDITIONS

(Handicap) of 10 sov. each, and 50 sov. extra unless forfeit be declared to Messrs. Weatherby and Sons, or to Messrs Pratt and Co., by Tuesday, January 31st, with an additional 15 sov. unless forfeit be so declared by Tuesday, March 7th, and a further 25 sov. unless forfeit be declared by Wednesday, March 22nd, to the Registry Office (Messrs. Weatherby and Sons) only, with 17,000 sov. added, being 5,000 sov. given by Messrs. Schweppes Ltd., 5,000 sov. by the Irish Hospitals' Sweepstakes, and 7,000 sov. (including a Gold Trophy value 600 sov.) by Messrs. Tophams Ltd.; second to receive 10%, third 5%, and fourth 2½% of the whole stakes for six yrs old and upwards which, up to the time of closing and since November 1st, 1957, have been placed first, second, third, or fourth by the Judge in a steeple chase of any distance at Aintree, Liverpool (this does not include such steeple chases run at the December Meeting on the Mildmay Course), or have won a steeple chase of three miles or upwards, of the advertised value of 400 sov. or with at least 300 sov. added to a sweepstakes (or the equivalent in foreign distances and money) or have won any steeple chase value 500 sov. to the winner (or the equivalent in foreign money), selling races in every case excepted; weights published January 26th; the highest weight to be not more than 12st. and the lowest weight not less than 10st; the GRAND NATIONAL COURSE, about four miles and 856 yards.

*.*The trainer of the winner will receive a cup value 100 sov. and the rider of the winner a cup value 50 sov.

In addition, 2,537 sov. given by Messrs. Schweppes Ltd., will be divided as follows:—

1,000 sov. to the Trainer of the winner	300 sov. to the Trainer of the second	100 sov. to the Trainer of the third	50 sov. to the Trainer of the fourth
*500 sov. to the Rider of the winner	*150 sov. to the Rider of the second	*50 sov. to the Rider of the third	*25 sov. to the Rider of the fourth
250 sov. to the Stable of the winner	75 sov. to the Stable of the second	25 sov. to the Stable of the third	12 sov. to the Stable of the fourth
*These prizes do not apply to Amateur Riders.	Trophies value 50 sov. (25 sov. in the case of the fourth) will be awarded in lieu.		

There will be a parade for this race
74 entries. Closed January 3rd, 1961.
Value to winner £18,270 2s. 6d.

Second £2,208 10s.	Third £1,104 5s.	Fourth £552 2s. 6d.

TOPHAMS LIMITED   **AINTREE RACECOURSE**   **LIVERPOOL**

while for the jockeys a medical team headed by six doctors is always on hand. Fully equipped ambulances, for both horses and humans, are much in evidence and can be dispatched within seconds to any point on the course.

In 1984 the maximum number of runners allowed to compete in the Grand National was limited to 40 for safety purposes, and in most races since then more runners have completed the course. When two horses tragically lost their lives at Becher's Brook in the 1989 National, an official enquiry was ordered by the Jockey Club and after many discussions involving the most eminent people involved in horse racing, the safety of animals and racecourse emergency facilities, its conclusions were published.

Acting upon the Jockey Club report promptly, alterations were made to three fences,

Above: A press release from Tophams Limited showing the modifications to the obstacles made for the 1961 Grand National

Far right: 'Well that's one way of looking at it!' The ever genial champion jockey Jonjo O'Neill takes a close-up view of The Chair

Right: Neil Cawthorne's action-packed painting of the Canal Turn in 1992 gives an excellent impression of the 90 degree left-handed turn immediately after the fence

with Becher's Brook receiving most attention. The outer running rail on the landing side of the obstacle was splayed back for several yards to allow more landing space for runners jumping in that area, but that was the less drastic action the famous obstacle was to face. The depth of the Brook was reduced and the much criticised steep bank which sloped back into it, levelled off with the intention of 'taking the sting out of Becher's Brook'.

More or less the same modifications were made to Valentine's Brook and the rail, fence and ditch adjacent to the Anchor Bridge, though neither of these obstacles has proved particularly treacherous for many years.

The most recent serious review of the Grand National course came about in 1993, as a result of the two false starts which led to that year's event being declared void. An improved starting gate mechanism was the result of those investigations and since its first use for the 1994 National, it has proved most successful.

With the emphasis very much on safety for horses and riders, Aintree Racecourse Company have left no stone

unturned or cost spared in its efforts to achieve this aim, fully aware that the reputation of the Grand National depends on that principle. Their task is made no easier by the various groups of so-called 'animal rights activists' who, although perhaps well-intentioned, are often misinformed concerning horse racing and appear determined to involve themselves in the way that Aintree organises its great steeplechase.

LIVERPOOL
and the NATIONAL

4

GRAND® NATIONAL
— AINTREE —

A CITY with two cathedrals, two tunnels under the River Mersey and two football teams of world renown, may seem overly endowed even without its being the home of the Beatles as well as a never ending abundance of comedians. In fact, ever eager to poke fun at themselves, Scousers will freely tell you that one needs to be a comedian merely to live in the place.

Yet their well-disguised inner pride is a legacy from forebears who knew only too well what it meant to suffer silently the indignity of unemployment, a humble acceptance of 'their place' in life and a grudging gratitude to any employer willing to offer the most menial opportunity to justify their existence. In essence they can truly be said to be the most down to earth people you could ever come across.

Left: Aerial view of the racecourse at Aintree

Liverpool as a seaport, twice within the space of 25 years, became the nation's lifeline, when two world wars threatened its freedom and existence. But with a cynicism bred by mistrust, its populace just got on with the job in the long-held hope that tomorrow could be no worse than today.

With the world's greatest steeplechase held on their doorstep, however, Liverpudlians fully appreciate the race which each spring provides their city with international recognition and they briefly revel in the limelight it generates. If, by chance, a son of the city ever ventures to have an opportunity of winning the race, nobody will be more vociferous than the inhabitants of Liverpool. One can but imagine the reaction to Crosby-based Mr Sirdefield winning that first Maghull Grand Liverpool Chase with THE DUKE in 1837 but his was merely the beginning of a quest by local inhabitants to achieve lasting recognition through success in the toughest race of all.

With the Grand National victory of GAMECOCK in 1887, Liverpool businessman Mr Thornewill fooled nobody with his registration of ownership as 'Mr Jay' and although returned at odds of 20/1, many money-lenders and pawnbrokers on Merseyside were forced to wipe certain slates clean. That loyal band of Liverpool gamblers hit the jackpot again in 1896 when local industrialist and benefactor William Hall-

Walker sent out his recent seven-year-old purchase THE SOARER to win the big race.

Another local man, Frank Bibby, led in the winner in 1905 when KIRKLAND was guided to a three-length victory by the Liverpool-born champion jockey Frank 'Tich' Mason.

By this time, Aintree racecourse was gaining fame as a venue for the latest wonder of the age of aviation. The vast open expanses of the racecourse provided ideal take-off and landing areas for the flimsy aircraft and for their fliers to test and improve their air-worthiness as well as their own flying techniques. Both local newspapers, the *Daily Post* and the *Mercury,* welcomed and encouraged these daring pioneers of powered flight and Sir William Pickles Hartley, whose famous jam-making factory was located at Aintree, offered £1,000 as a prize for the first successful flight from there to Manchester. Most fancied among the many famous aviators competing was the American Colonel Samuel Cody, who transported his bi-plane in sections from Doncaster, re-assembled it at Aintree and flew as far as Eccleston Park before calling it a day when hampered by fog. Some three months after Frank Bibby scored his second National victory with the one-eyed GLENSIDE, a Liverpool-born airman named Henry Melly made the Manchester flight from Aintree in July 1911 in 49 minutes, accompanied by one of the first women ever to fly in Britain, his wife Ellen. Flying against a headwind, they made the return journey in 65 minutes and from then on regular flying exhibitions were conducted at Aintree, with the ever popular Colonel Cody often pitting his skill against such well known fliers as the Brazilian Alberto Santos Dumont, Scotsman James More and the Reverend Sidney Swann who was Rector of nearby Crosby.

During the First World War the National Aircraft Factory was established alongside the racecourse, turning out large numbers of Bristol aircraft for the newly-formed Royal Flying Corps, which before being turned over to the military underwent flight tests around the area. By the mid-1920s, air travel had become a regular means of transport and on 30 April 1924 the Liverpool to Belfast airmail service was inaugurated, with aircraft flying from and to Aintree's landing ground on a daily basis.

In 1925 the Grand National was won again by a Liverpool owner, cotton broker David Gould, whose gelding DOUBLE CHANCE was ridden to victory by Major John Philip Wilson, who most appropriately had shot down an enemy Zeppelin over Hull while a member of the Royal Flying Corps.

Another member of the Liverpool Cotton Exchange, Mr WH Midwood, experienced the delight of leading in the winner of the race in 1930 when SHAUN GOILIN held on in a very close finish to succeed by a neck from MELLERAY'S BELLE and SIR LINDSAY.

By the time the next National came around there was greater speculation centred on the race than ever before, as a result of an announcement to the effect that the Irish Hospital Sweepstakes were to hold their first lottery on the event. With the prize-money offered reaching levels hitherto undreamt of, millions of tickets were sold, of which one was purchased by an immigrant Italian waiter named Emilio Scala who lived in Battersea Park Road, London. After the draw was made some weeks before the race by a team of nurses in Dublin, the newspapers published long lists of those fortunate enough to have drawn a horse and with each of these guaranteed a prize of some value, the outcome of the race was eagerly awaited.

Making his fifth appearance in the race, the nine-year-old gelding GRAKLE was thought to have had his best chance when finishing sixth in the race two years before, but even so was well supported in the betting. Owned by Mr Cecil Taylor of the Liverpool Corn Exchange, GRAKLE was trained by the famous Tom Coulthwaite and ridden by Bob Lyall, whose brother Frank had finished second in the race in 1912. Away to a good start on perfect going, the 1931 Grand

National field of 43 runners suffered few falls in the early part of the race and with former winners GREGALACH and SHAUN GOILIN among the leaders over the Water Jump, both the favourite EASTER HERO and GRAKLE were in prominent positions. After the second Becher's, GREGALACH and GREAT SPAN disputed the lead for several fences before GRAKLE began making ground on them both. Leading over the last, GRAKLE ran on to win by a length and a half from GREGALACH with ANNANDALE third and last year's hero SHAUN GOILIN sixth.

Winning owner Mr Taylor very generously sent £50 as a present to jockey Tim Hamey for, as Taylor said in his letter, 'showing GRAKLE how to get round Aintree two years ago'. The winner's prize-money amounted to £9,385, which was somewhat less than the £354,544 the Italian waiter Emilio Scala received for drawing GRAKLE in the Irish Hospital Sweepstakes.

A very popular day out for all Merseysiders had been for many years the annual inspection of the Grand National course the Sunday before the big race, known affectionately as 'Jump Sunday'. With the fences fully dressed, flagged and ready for the great contest to be decided over them in just a few days, thousands upon thousands of visitors walked the course free of charge, gazing questioningly at the size of each fence while fully aware of the dangers they presented. In a carnival-like atmosphere the throngs strolled, inspecting the sideshows, amateur escapologists and an army of tipsters each with the promise they could tell you the winner, for a price. But always the attention would be drawn back to those huge spruce barriers whose dimensions made it impossible to see beyond. To the detriment of all who welcomed and enjoyed Jump

Above: The traditional Jump Sunday tour of the Grand National fences was a popular day out for many thousands of people

Right: Local owner Mr Noel Le Mare with his triple National winner and the pride of Merseyside, RED RUM

Sunday, the custom was brought to an end in the early 1970s as a result of persistent damage to the racecourse by a small group of hooligans.

With racing at Aintree coming to an end after the 1940 Grand National because of the Second World War, the place became home to many thousands of allied troops, and initially some of those evacuated from the beaches of Dunkirk were based there in transit while they were re-equipped and formed into new companies. With America entering the war after the Japanese attack on Pearl Harbour in December 1941, countless numbers of infantrymen from across the Atlantic were billeted in the various stable blocks on the racecourse, as part of the long preparation for the allied invasion of occupied Europe. Through all those years the Stars and Stripes flag of the United States of America flew proudly above Aintree's historic County Stand.

In the post-war rush to repair the ravages of war inflicted on much of Britain, many new construction companies were formed and one of the most prosperous of these came to be the Liverpool based North West Construction company, owned by Mr Noel Le Mare. His was a true rags-to-riches tale of success, for when still a long way from being the wealthy man he became, he set himself three ambitions for his future life. The first was that he should become a millionaire; the second to marry a beautiful woman, and the third was that he should own a

winner of the Grand National. Through his own hard work, enterprise and selectivity, Mr Le Mare achieved both the first two but as with many people before and since, the dream of Aintree glory proved the most elusive. In 1969 his FURORE II gave a good account of himself in the race, showing prominently for most of the way before eventually finishing eighth behind HIGHLAND WEDDING. With a determination and persistence which had served him so well in the world of business, the ageing Noel Le Mare eventually found both the horse and the man to provide him with the one remaining success he craved. RED RUM and Donald McCain, the man who purchased and trained him on behalf of Mr Le Mare, not only completely re-wrote the record books but in doing so made that long-held dream of Le Mare's a reality, three times over. During the heady five years of RED RUM'S virtual domination of the National scene, Liverpudlians shared the pride of his achievements as if they all had a personal involvement with the horse. Well, of course, in the convoluted reasoning unique to inhabitants of this city, they did; for was it not 'de Pool' which provided 'Rummy' with the place to perform his record-breaking deeds?

Rarely considered a place of culture, Liverpool none the less can lay claim to having one the finest philharmonic orchestras in the the world, an abundance of art galleries, museums and in recent years at least, has become one of the nation's major tourist attractions. Famed throughout the world by now is the always well-attended Beatles Weekend, and with the ancient docklands receiving a new lease of life in the most imaginative manner, the Maritime Museum amid the intrinsically beautiful Albert Dock complex is a worthy tribute to a city whose fame was earned by seafarers.

It was way back in the mid-nineteenth century when a local brewer became mayor of Liverpool for the second time and made the decision to donate a means of appreciating the wonders of the art world to the people of Liverpool. His Liverpool Art Gallery was a bold and generous step at a time when things were extremely hard for all but the very wealthy. Undaunted, Mr Walker, together with many other social benefactors including Mr Lee Jones who instituted boys clubs for working-class youths, pursued his intention energetically and purposefully. His son, Colonel William-Hall Walker, subsequently followed his father's example as a man intent on improving the lot of the less privileged.

An enthusiastic and most talented horseman himself, William Hall-Walker in 1896 purchased a runner in the Grand National barely six weeks before the race, from a serving officer in the 9th Lancers, David Campbell. Stationed at the Curragh in Ireland, David Campbell was also Liverpool born and insisted as part of the sale agreement that he be allowed to ride the horse in the forthcoming National.

Receiving very generous odds against his horse THE SOARER, Mr Hall-Walker wagered heavily, possibly more from sentiment than anything else, but with David Campbell riding a brilliant race on the seven-year-old, THE SOARER won by one and a half lengths from former winner FATHER O'FLYNN. More than content with the prestige attached to winning the race, William Hall-Walker gave all the proceeds of his gambling investments on THE SOARER to extending the Liverpool Art Gallery instituted by his father and to buying

in more art treasures. As a mark of appreciation, the establishment was named the Walker Art Gallery and today remains one of the finest of its kind in the whole of Europe.

David Campbell, having emblazoned his name forever on Aintree's Roll of Honour, concentrated his future exploits very firmly on his military career and by the time of his death at the age of 67 in 1936, Lt-General Sir David Campbell, KCB, had become one the most highly decorated men in British military history. William Hall-Walker engrossed himself in public service, becoming Member of Parliament for Widnes and also involving himself in his dearest pursuit, the breeding of thoroughbred bloodstock. After purchasing many acres of land in Kildare, Hall-Walker set up the Tully Stud from which was leased by King Edward VII a colt bred there called MINORU which in 1909 won the Epsom Derby in the Royal colours. During the dark days of 1915, with British morale at a low ebb through reversals suffered in the Great War, Colonel Hall-Walker presented the Tully Stud, together with all its brood mares and stallions, to the nation and it became known as the National Stud. Elected to the peerage in 1920 and also to the Jockey Club, William Hall-Walker became Lord

Wavertree and the following year his horse ALL WHITE was remounted by jockey Bob Chadwick to finish a distant third in the Grand National. Lord Wavertree died in 1933 at the age of 66, leaving all his many racing trophies and paintings of his famous thoroughbreds to the Corporation of Liverpool.

Among those other classically designed buildings lining the north side of William Brown Street, stands Liverpool's County Museum just two buildings away from the Walker Art Gallery. Both form part of a number of such establishments in the area under the control of National Museums and Galleries on Merseyside and for three months during 1989 an international exhibition took place at the Museum marking the 150th anniversary of the Grand National. Displaying an abundance of rare, valuable and interesting trophies, paintings and general memorabilia associated with the famous steeplechase, many hundreds of thousands of people visited the exhibition. The list of

contributors included owners, trainers, jockeys, Her Majesty The Queen, Her Majesty Queen Elizabeth The Queen Mother, and Mr Paul Mellon, the wealthy American who sent over a number of artefacts from his racing museum in the United States. Following its success, a smaller though permanent Grand National display was included in the newly installed Museum of Liverpool Life at Liverpool's popular Albert Dock complex in 1993.

It was, of course, in that year of 1993 that an error in the starting apparatus at Aintree led to two false starts, a 'Grand National that never was', and that contest being declared void. Apart from the two world wars, it remains the only occasion when no winner's name has been included on Aintree's Roll of Honour for a specific year.

If humour, sadness and anger were a mixture of sentiments provoked by affairs at Aintree in 1993, it was most certainly the former which took precedence twelve months later.

As one of the younger generation of famous Liverpool comedians, the zany Freddie Starr followed a long tradition of local comic geniuses, embellished by such household names as Tommy Handley, Derek Guyler, Ted Ray, Arthur Askey and the irrepressible 'Squire of Knotty Ash' himself, Ken Dodd. Although not present at the 1994 Grand National due to television commitments, Freddie Starr was ably represented in the race by the Richard Dunwoody-ridden ten-year-old MIINNEHOMA. After something of a disappointing career over fences, the gelding's jumping had given rise to concern and after running unplaced behind the French horse THE FELLOW in the Cheltenham Gold Cup, MIINNEHOMA lined up at Aintree a comparatively lightly raced horse. Giving a perfect example of horsemanship on very heavy ground, Richard Dunwoody considerably kept

Far left: Richard Dunwoody provides popular Liverpool comedian Freddie Starr with Grand National fame by winning the 1994 race while notching up his second riding success in the event

Left: Stranded, bewildered but undaunted, many thousands found great kindness and generosity from the local people in their hours of need in 1997

his mount just off the pace in the early stages of the race while keeping well within striking distance of the leaders, but at Becher's Brook second time all his efforts almost came to nought. MIINNEHOMA pitched so badly on landing over the notorious Brook that his nose actually scraped the ground, but with a skill derived from natural brilliance, inherent dedication and a technique honed to perfection, Richard Dunwoody kept his place in the saddle, corrected his mount's error and miraculously kept his horse in the race. Revealing all the attributes which had gained him not only the jockey championship but a worldwide reputation for excellence, Dunwoody gauged his challenge to a nicety, coming clear from the final fence to win by a length and a quarter from JUST SO, with the favourite MOORCROFT BOY twenty lengths back in third place. Ever the showman and despite his absence, successful owner Freddie Starr somehow made telephone contact with BBC presenter Desmond Lynam to congratulate both trainer Martin Pipe and particularly the superb Richard Dunwoody, who eight years after his first success in the race on WEST TIP had once again shown them all the way home.

If the race so long proudly held in the highest regard by the citizens of Liverpool could ever have repaid such attachment, that opportunity came under the most frightening circumstances on Grand National day in 1997.

From that one single terrorist attempt to terrify and intimidate decent, law-abiding people about to watch a piece of sporting history being made, the inhabitants of Liverpool at last became recognised throughout the world as caring, sympathetic and extremely decent people; prepared at any time to open their arms and hearts to anyone in a time of abject crisis. Described by a media so often critical of Merseysiders as displaying the spirit of Dunkirk and the Blitz, the exceptional behaviour of the many thousands of Liverpool people in giving succour to the stranded and weary racegoers over that long Aintree weekend was really also something else. Quite simply, it was the spirit of Liverpool itself.

AINTREE

This plaque was commissioned by
Aintree Racecourse Company Ltd
as a mark of the Company's gratitude
to all local residents who showed
such warm hospitality to racegoers
in need of help in the aftermath of the
events of Saturday 5th April 1997
This plaque was unveiled by
Aintree Racecourse's Managing Director.
Mr. Charles Barnett
on September 12th 1997

Left: In appreciation of Liverpool people's magnificent response on that worrying day in 1997, Aintree Racecourse Company erected this plaque on the outer wall of the jockey's room

Far left: The mass evacuation of the racecourse after the bomb threat in 1997

MONARCHY
and the NATIONAL

5

GRAND® NATIONAL
— AINTREE —

THE NATIONAL AND THE BRITISH ROYAL FAMILY are inextricably linked, but it is at Royal Ascot in mid-summer that the Royals will always be found celebrating the annual fixture which attracts the finest flat racehorses to be found anywhere. Suggested as an ideal location for a racecourse by Queen Anne after a drive across 'Ascott Common' one day in 1711, it was she who founded the race meeting which has become one of the outstanding features of the British Turf. To this day the opening event at Royal Ascot remains the Queen Anne Stakes over one mile, in memory of the lady whose carriage-bound journey from the gates of Windsor Great Park led to Ascot becoming a major venue for racing.

Left: Accompanied by her trainer Peter Cazalet, Her Majesty Queen Elizabeth The Queen Mother and Princess Margaret inspect the National runners in the paddock in 1965

Still further back in time, during the reign of Queen Elizabeth I, horses were raced at a variety of places, including the area now known as Merseyside, and one of the earliest to be recorded was the contest for the Crosby Bell in 1577. This event, run on the foreshore at Crosby, appears to have been instigated by the donor of the silver bell, Mr Edward Torbock, with the condition that it be 'A challenge trophy competed for by horses every year on Ascencion Day for ever'.

Two years after the 1837 coronation of Queen Victoria, LOTTERY won the first Grand Liverpool Steeplechase held at Aintree and it was Her Majesty's eldest son Albert Edward, Prince of Wales, who became the first heir to the throne for many years to take an active part in horse racing. Born at Buckingham Palace on 9 November 1841, he was 38 years of age and already a father himself when his colours were carried in a steeplechase for the first time. Following the tradition of military officers anxious to be represented in a regimental race, HRH The Prince of Wales employed the services of his close friend Lord Marcus Beresford in selecting a jumper suitable for the purpose. Chosen well by a man who was more than a little familiar with the sport of 'racing between the flags', the brown gelding LEONIDAS provided His Royal Highness with a successful introduction to steeplechasing by winning the Military Hunt Steeplechase at Aldershot on 14 April 1880. Although this was the first recognised involvement of the Prince of Wales in cross-country racing, a little over twelve months earlier in 1879 a certain horse called JACKAL finished second in the Grand National under the light blue and black capped colours of Lord Marcus Beresford. The horse was in fact jointly owned by His Lordship and the Prince of Wales.

In March 1882 Prince Edward gained a victory at Sandown Park which gave him particular satisfaction, the race being the Household Brigade Cup over three miles, confined to owners and riders who were serving officers in the Household Brigade. In a very close finish, the Royal

challenger FAIR PLAY won by a neck from SHABBINGTON, having been beautifully ridden by Mr Luke White, who after a brilliant military career became Lord Annaly.

A son of Derby winner BLAIR ATHOL, the gelding THE SCOT was the next important purchase made by Lord Marcus on behalf of Prince Edward and after finishing third on the continent in the Great Baden Steeplechase of 1883, was prepared for the following year's Grand National. Starting 6/1 favourite at Aintree in 1884, THE SCOT was among the leaders right from the start, coping well with the tricky fences and showing great promise when a close-up second over the Water Jump at the end of the first circuit. Still well in contention, THE SCOT came down at the second Canal Turn and after making his challenge at the last fence, the six-year-old VOLUPTUARY raced clear to win by four lengths from FRIGATE and ROQUEFORT. Although the patriotic spectators at Aintree that day were disappointed at not witnessing the Royal victory they'd expected, the winner had in fact a very close connection with the Royal household. VOLUPTUARY had been bred in 1878 at Hampton Court by Her Majesty Queen Victoria, was purchased by Lord Rosebery and after winning the Dee Stakes on the flat at Chester, led the field around Tattenham Corner in the 1881 Epsom Derby before finishing among the also-rans. His success in the National was all the more praise-worthy in being the first steeplechase VOLUPTUARY had ever taken part in.

Subsequently sold to the well-known actor Leonard Boyne, VOLUPTUARY left the hurly-burly, perilous uncertainty of the turf to take up a new career as a most important member of the cast in the play *The Prodigal Daughter*. Appearing every night on the stage of the Drury Lane Theatre, the gelding displayed his jumping prowess by leaping an artificial water jump in the drama, which required his partner Mr Boyne to fall into the water. For performing this rather athletic indignity, the actor was paid an extra five shillings.

It was not until 1887 that the Prince of Wales acquired another steeplechaser, the huge seventeen hands high HOHENLINDEN, with which he hoped to win the principal race the Grand Military Gold Cup at Sandown Park's Grand Military meeting. Ridden by the immensely talented amateur Captain Roddy Owen, HOHENLINDEN duly won the race but no sooner had His Royal Highness been heartily cheered by the delighted crowds, than it was announced that an objection had been made to the winner by the owner of the second horse. The conditions of the race required that all horses competing be owned by army officers on full pay and as the owner of HOHENLINDEN was not an officer on active service, the Stewards had no alternative but to uphold the objection and disqualify the horse. After winning three races on the trot the following season, the horse was presented to the Shah of Persia as 'a fine specimen of an English hunter'.

Again with the assistance of Lord Marcus Beresford, the Prince of Wales became the owner of two likely Aintree prospects in the form of MAGIC and the younger HETTIE. The former, although at long odds, ran a good enough race in the 1888 Grand National to finish in eighth place behind the winner PLAYFAIR. By way of consolation, MAGIC romped home to win the Grand Sefton Chase at Aintree that November and within days carried off the Prince of Wales' Steeplechase at Derby in very heavy going. HETTIE joined MAGIC as a competitor for their Royal owner in the big Aintree test of 1889 and though failing to complete the course, MAGIC once more got round, this time in fifth place behind the mare FRIGATE who won the race at her sixth attempt.

Always a dabbler in the affairs of man, it was fate alone which brought the heir to the English throne into contact with a certain Tommy Lushington. A most accomplished horseman, described by no less a judge of rider than George Lambton as 'the crack amateur of the day', Kent-born though Irish-domiciled Lushington was also a very accomplished

manager and trainer of racehorses. After riding SAFETY-PIN to victory for the Prince of Wales in the Andover Stakes at Stockbridge in 1896, he was asked by His Royal Highness to look out for any steeplechasers which he felt may prove worthy of carrying the Royal colours. So successful did the purchases he made on behalf of the Prince prove to be that Mr Lushington was employed to train and manage the jumpers belonging to the Prince of Wales in Ireland.

By pure coincidence, however, it was another Kentish-born trainer who provided the future monarch with his first big winner on the Turf. Richard Marsh, having been entrusted with the care of his flat racehorses in 1892, sent out PERSIMMON from his Newmarket headquarters four years later to win both the Epsom Derby and the Doncaster St Leger for the Prince of Wales. Another classic fell to the Royal owner that season when the filly THAIS carried off the One Thousand Guineas at Newmarket.

Yet, across the Irish Sea Tommy Lushington had discovered a young horse called AMBUSH II which he felt certain would develop into the kind of staying chaser His Royal Highness

Above: AMBUSH II begins the long run to the post in the 1900 National to become the only winner of the race owned by a member of the Royal Family

Left: The 1884 winner VOLUPTUARY was bred by Her Majesty Queen Victoria and subsequently appeared on the stage of the Drury Lane Theatre in a play. It was in this year that His Royal Highness The Prince of Wales was represented for the first time in the race, his horse THE SCOT failing to complete the course

sought. Purchased for 500 guineas, the gelding carried the Royal colours to victory on his second outing in 1898, over four miles at Punchestown, and before the end of the season triumphed again, this time at Leopardstown. So pleased were both trainer and owner with their new pupil, the decision was taken to enter AMBUSH II in the 1899 Grand National, a most ambitious move for by the time the race was to be run, the gelding would still only be a five-year-old.

The horse's sole race before arriving at Aintree in late March 1899 was appropriately the Prince of Wales' Steeplechase over three and a half miles at Sandown Park on 10 February. With a perfect display of jumping, AMBUSH II won convincingly by eight lengths, with previous National winners THE SOARER and DROGHEDA among the eight opponents he defeated. Third in the betting for the Grand National behind two extremely brilliant horses, GENTLE IDA and MANIFESTO, the Royal contender coped well with the unusual fences but from the second Canal Turn was unable to keep pace with the leaders. In finishing in seventh place behind the mighty MANIFESTO, who was recording his

second victory in the race, AMBUSH II had, however, given a wonderful performance for such a young and inexperienced horse. This view was also obviously taken by the handicapper, who for the next Grand National raised him fifteen pounds in the weights to eleven stone three pounds.

On a bright, clear spring afternoon on the first Grand National day of the twentieth century, the future King of England took his place in the Aintree paddock with fifteen other owners, all with their private hopes, fears and dreams of the gigantic test ahead. Ridden as the previous year cautiously by Algy Anthony, who assisted Tommy Lushington in training the horse, AMBUSH II was kept clear of trouble towards the rear of the field on the first circuit, but after jumping the Water Jump began making progress. Jumping Becher's for the final time, AMBUSH II was within striking distance of the leading group and when he jumped to the front over the Canal Turn, a huge patriotic roar rose from that furthest point of the course. The cheers suddenly increased after Valentine's Brook, though, when that grand old favourite MANIFESTO took issue with the Royal challenger. Coming back on to the racecourse

with just two jumps left, MANIFESTO was in front and seemed set fair for an incredible third victory in the race he had graced for so long. Cheering till their throats throbbed, the vast crowd's loyalties were totally divided when AMBUSH II put in a renewed effort between the last two fences and landing first on the flat, made good his weight advantage of 24 pounds. Staying on to win by four lengths, AMBUSH II passed the post in front of the fast finishing BARSAC, who got up on the line to deprive MANIFESTO of second place by a neck. The latter was conceding a merciless 43 pounds to the horse which finished a neck in front of him.

With emotions running high, the Prince of Wales went on to the racecourse to welcome home the horse who had given him one of his happiest moments in racing. There were, though, other celebrations to come for the sporting Prince in that first year of the new century. His colt DIAMOND JUBILEE, whose headstrong waywardness on the racecourse could only be controlled by an unknown stable-lad named Herbert Jones, carried off racing's triple crown of Two Thousand Guineas, Derby and St Leger before the end of the season.

Upon the death of Her Majesty Queen Victoria on 22 January 1901, the sporting Prince Albert Edward, who was the most respected man on the British Turf, became King Edward VII and with the court in mourning and other more serious matters of State to concern himself with, severely curtailed his racing activities.

In the 1903 Grand National AMBUSH II was well in contention when falling at the last fence, and the following year made an early exit at the third fence in the race won by the New Zealand-bred MOIFAA. MANIFESTO finished eighth in that 1904 National, his last appearance in the race, as also it was for AMBUSH II. In order to have a runner in the 1905

Aintree event, King Edward VII purchased the most recent National victor MOIFAA but despite starting favourite, the horse failed to complete the course. His Majesty's last chance to savour again the unique thrill of leading in the winner of the National came in 1908, but sadly his representative FLAXMAN could do no better than finish fourth behind the surprise winner RUBIO.

Ironically, it a was a colt bred by Liverpool-born William Hall-Walker which provided the King with what was to be his final great moment on the Turf. MINORU, leased to him by Hall-Walker, won the 1909 Epsom Derby for His Majesty, who after a short illness died on 6 May 1910 at the age of 68. One of the most fitting and poignant aspects of the funeral of Edward the Peacemaker, was his ceremonial charger following the King's gun-carriage-born coffin through the streets of London on the way to his final resting place. With the King's boots reversed in the stirrups the horse, the aforementioned MOIFAA, far from his birthplace on the other side of the world, kept the even pace of the procession, noticeably with his noble head bowed.

Although both King George V and his successor King Edward VIII were regular visitors to Aintree on its day of days, it was not until 1950 that a Royal runner again took part in a Grand National. Her Majesty Queen Elizabeth having been encouraged to become the owner of a steeplechaser by that tremendous ambassador of jumping Lord Mildmay, watched excitedly as her gelding MONAVEEN

was among the leaders approaching the end of the first circuit in the 1950 National. Making his one mistake at the thirteenth fence, MONAVEEN lost his position and was among the stragglers going back into the country. Staying on well, though, he gradually worked his way through the field to finish an honourable fifth behind that great Liverpool horse FREEBOOTER.

Now known and loved as Her Majesty Queen Elizabeth The Queen Mother, that most gracious of all Royal ladies has become, not just the most respected owner in National Hunt racing, but more importantly someone whose involvement with the sport has increased its attraction beyond all expectations. If ever the genuine spirit of true sportsmanship was displayed, it was that dramatic moment in 1956 when Her Majesty's DEVON LOCH raced clear from the last fence in the National towards 'certain' victory. Still painful and inexplicable to all who sadly witnessed it, DEVON LOCH's collapse to the ground when within 50 yards of victory must now read like a piece of fiction from the pen of the jockey who shared the trauma, Dick Francis. Yet hiding her disappointment, the Queen Mother's first act after satisfying herself that her jockey and DEVON LOCH had suffered no injury, was to

Above: On the occasion of the first Royal Grand National competitor for 42 years, King George VI attends Aintree with Queen Elizabeth to watch her runner MONAVEEN take part. With them in the paddock is Lord Mildmay, on the right, and Royal jockey Tony Grantham

Right: Just seconds from despair! An ecstatic Royal party on the roof of the County Stand cheering DEVON LOCH on to 'victory'

congratulate the connections of the horse who must surely be the luckiest winner ever, E.S.B.

If victory in the Grand National has always eluded her, Her Majesty has achieved Aintree success over the big fences with both INCH ARRAN and that so reliable equine servant SILVER DOME. In 1991, those assembled for the last Seagram Grand National had their final opportunity to welcome her when she officially opened Aintree's latest construction, The Queen Mother Stand.

Following in her grandmother's footsteps, Her Royal Highness The Princess Royal has openly displayed her fondness of Liverpool's best known racing day by becoming a regular visitor and even a competitor at the racecourse. On Grand National day in 1987, the Princess Royal rode her own horse CNOC NA CUILLE into sixth place behind NEWLIFE CONNECTION in the two and a half mile White Satin Steeplechase over Aintree's Mildmay fences, and twelve months later she returned to the racecourse to perform a very special function. She unveiled Aintree's tribute to the greatest of all racing legends, the RED RUM statue, opposite the entrance to The Queen Mother Stand, which was sculptured by former jockey Philip

Blacker who four times finished behind 'Rummy' in the National.

Again principal guest of honour for the 150th running of the race in 1997, the Princess Royal was caught up in the evacuation of the racecourse after the bomb scare. Undaunted, however, she was back at Aintree 48 hours later to witness LORD GYLLENE romp home and to present the trophies to the winner's connections. In her honour the latest addition to Aintree's skyline, The Princess Royal Stand, was named and officially opened by her on the eve of the big race in 1998.

Above: When the roar of the crowd was silenced. Barely 50 yards from a well-deserved victory, DEVON LOCH inexplicably slithers to the ground and out of the race

Left: An emotional return to Aintree in 1991 when the Queen Mother performed the opening ceremony of the new grandstand named in her honour. She is accompanied by Racecourse Chairman, The Honourable Peter Greenall

FAMILY AFFAIRS

THROUGHOUT THE HISTORY

of the Grand National, one of the most enduring patterns associated with the event has been that of various generations of families who have endeavoured to secure distinction in the most gruelling race of all. Relationships are a fundamental element of 'The Romance of the National'. Undoubtedly romance played a major role in the victory of LOTTERY in 1839, with jockey Jem Mason soon after marrying the daughter of the man who owned the horse, a Miss Elmore.

Left: 1935 winner
REYNOLDSTOWN is led in and
the Furlong family can
begin their celebrations

When William Archer rode LITTLE CHARLEY to a four-length victory in the 1858 Grand National, his youngest son Frederick James was just fourteen months old and Liverpool was to become the scene of many of Fred Archer's innumerable triumphs which labelled him the greatest flat-race jockey of all time. Extending the family's tradition, Frederick Charles Archer, grandson of the Grand National winning jockey and nephew of flat-race genius Fred, became a trainer of some repute before the Great War. While serving as a trooper with the Royal Buckinghamshire Yeomanry during that conflict, he became a close friend of Captain Anthony de Rothschild who, when peace was restored, made Archer a present of a horse called DOUBLE CHANCE. Of little account on the flat and after developing some leg problems, the gelding was gradually restored to fitness by Frederick Archer to become a most reliable jumper. Shortly before the 1925 Grand National, a half share in the horse was sold to the Liverpool cotton broker David Gould and it was in his colours that DOUBLE CHANCE produced a devastating late turn of speed to win the race by four lengths from the favourite OLD TAY BRIDGE. Subsequently appointed private trainer to Lord Glanely, Frederick Charles Archer was sadly killed in a car crash in 1928. In his will he thoughtfully made provision to ensure the future well-being of DOUBLE CHANCE by leaving an amount of money for the care of his National 'gift horse'.

A tragic occurrence also overshadowed the involvement of young James Wynne in the 1862 Grand National when, coincidentally, only thirteen runners faced the starter. Son of Denis Wynne, who rode MATTHEW to become the first Irish-trained winner fifteen years before, James longed to experience the thrill his father had known during his fine career over the mighty Liverpool fences. That Grand National of 1862 began for the whole Wynne family in the most appalling way, with the sad news that the young Irish jockey's sister had died suddenly at home. With commendable compassion, owner Lord de Freyne attempted to persuade the young man not to ride his horse O'CONNELL in the big race but knowing his sister shared his pride in making a first attempt at the contest their father had won, James Wynne insisted on fulfilling his commitment. In full view of the stands at the plain fence before the Water Jump, O'CONNELL was brought down by a fallen horse and in the mêlée which followed, James received internal injuries from which he died later that evening.

The dual success accomplished by Lord Coventry as the owner of full sisters EMBLEM and EMBLEMATIC in 1863 and 1864 most certainly had a serious influence on His Lordship's cousin, Captain Henry Coventry of the Grenadier Guards. Engaged to ride the five-year-old ALCIBIADE, who had never taken part in a public steeplechase, 23-year-old Captain

Coventry was most unkindly referred to by certain pundits as a 'swell from the Guards who no doubt prepared for such an event on a diet of anchovy toast, varied with devilled biscuits, washed down by unlimited champagne, with big cigars in between as a soother'. On a bright clear day, with a fine covering of snow on the course, Henry Coventry set about making his critics eat their words. Keeping his mount to the wide outside all the way round, the 'swell from the Guards' had ALCIBIADE perfectly balanced at every obstacle and challenging the leader HALL COURT at the final flight of hurdles, produced a finish which was to be talked about long after the result. With both horses neck-to-neck up that soul-destroying run to the line, Captain Coventry rode like a demon possessed to bring ALCIBIADE first past the post, a meagre head in front of HALL COURT. The gallant and very talented Captain Coventry made his first Grand National a winning one and also his last. He never rode in the race again and with genuine eloquence apologised to his uncle Lord Coventry for beating his Lordship's EMBLEMATIC, the favourite, into third place.

In terms of consistently outstanding riding, the Beasley brothers reigned supreme at Aintree from the late 1870s until the early 1890s. It was the eldest son of the Irish family Thomas who first ventured across the Irish Sea for a tilt at the National. Unplaced aboard SULTANA in the race in 1877, Tommy Beasley looked certain to win the following year when partnering the 20/1 chance MARTHA but the mare

tired close to home to be beaten by two lengths by SHIFNAL. Stimulated by their brother's performance, a concerted attack was launched on Aintree in 1879 by all four Beasley brothers: Tommy, Harry, Willie and John. Born and bred at Atley, County Kildare, they were horsemen of the highest calibre and with Tommy attached to the powerful yard of trainer Henry Eyre Linde, each of his younger brothers were set a powerful example. In that National, the only one in which four brothers from the same family have competed, Tommy finished third on MARTHA, Willie eighth with LORD MARCUS and Harry came in ninth with TURCO. John Beasley pulled up his mount VICTOR during the course of the race. Tommy Beasley's record in the Grand National will stand comparison with the finest of riders of any era – from twelve rides in the race he won it three times, was second twice and once third, and only twice failed to get round. Equally adept on the flat, he won the Irish Derby twice and at the height of his prowess rode WHISPER LOW to victory in the Grande Steeplechase de Paris in 1882. Harry took part in thirteen Nationals, winning it astride COME AWAY in 1891, finishing twice second and once third, with victories also in the Grande Steeplechase de Paris in 1883 on TOO GOOD and ROYAL MEATH in 1890. Aintree was also the scene of a record four triumphs for Harry Beasley in the Grand Sefton Steeplechase with JUPITER JONAS, LORD CHANCELLOR, ZITELLA and ST GEORGE.

His final steeplechase winner was in the four-mile Kildare Hunt Cup at Punchestown in 1918, although he continued riding on the flat for many years until winning Baldoyle's Corinthian Plate in 1935 at the age 85. A full 70 years after Harry's victory on COME AWAY, his grandson Bobby Beasley won the 1961 Grand National riding only the second grey to succeed in the race, NICOLAUS SILVER. A worthy footnote to that very remarkable Kildare family named Beasley.

It was again from that mystical land across the Irish Sea, that in 1895 a besotted young man named Joseph Widger brought to reality a dream held by many though realised by few. Virtually bred to be a horseman of renown, Joe was born in 1864 in Waterford, into a family famous as horse dealers who supplied remounts to the cavalry regiments of most European countries. Riding his first winner over fences when barely fourteen years of age at Bangor, after absconding from school, Joe Widger and his brother John bought a horse in 1893 with the somewhat cumbersome name of WILD MAN FROM BORNEO. Within twelve months Joe rode it into third place in the National. Finishing less than two lengths behind the winner WHY NOT, 'The Wild Man' gave the whole Widger family the confidence that 1895 was going to be a year for a mighty celebration. The going was extremely heavy at Aintree on National day and

Above: 105 years after Joe Widger's moment of Aintree glory, his great-grand-nephew, the up and coming professional Robert Widger, takes CHOISTY to the start of the 2000 Grand National

Right: The younger son of a Welsh veterinary surgeon, Fred Rees brings SHAUN SPADAH home alone in the 1921 race. Only three others remounted to complete the course

displaying a wisdom way beyond his years, Joe Widger adroitly preserved his mount's energy all through the first circuit and for much of the final round. Approaching Valentine's Brook, WILD MAN FROM BORNEO was taken up to match strides with the leading pair, CATHAL and MANIFESTO. Staying in touch, Joe Widger left his challenge until after jumping the last fence in third place. Responding immediately to his rider's demands, WILD MAN FROM BORNEO swept to the front to win cleverly by a length and a half from CATHAL, with VAN DER BERG, MANIFESTO and WHY NOT nearest of the remainder. With beacons burning on the hills around Waterford, the celebrations continued well into many nights and at the Tower Hotel in the city 100 years later, the centenary festival organised by over 300 descendants of the original Widger family relived their ancestors'

moments of joy. In 1999 a highly talented young man named Robert Widger revived family memories of his great-grand-uncle Joe, who began their National quest, by riding CHOISTY in the race. Partnering the horse again in the 2000 contest, Robert Widger has carried his family name proudly into the 21st century.

After guiding home over 300 winners in France and Belgium during his youth, Ernie Piggott eventually settled in England to become champion jockey in 1910, 1913 and 1915. Riding the twelve stone seven pounds top weight JERRY M to victory in the 1912 Grand National improved on his previous best effort when finishing third on the great MANIFESTO ten years before. Carrying the same weight burden at the top of the handicap in 1919, Piggott again made light of his task to bring home the favourite POETHLYN by a comfortable eight lengths, shortly after which he retired from the saddle to set up as a trainer at the Old Manor House in Letcombe Regis. Both his sons, Keith and Victor, rode in the National during the 1920s without gaining the prestige gained by their father, but in 1963 Keith saddled the 66/1 shock winner of the race AYALA. His son was, of course, the incomparable Lester Piggott who, as already chronicled, rode many winners on the flat at Aintree. During the 1980s Lester's daughter Maureen was involved in a BBC television exercise which saw her riding over the National fences. With a small camera fitted to her hat, Maureen recorded a close-up view of the obstacles her great-grandfather twice successfully raced over and in so doing became the fourth generation of the famous family to ride at Aintree.

Of all the many fine riders to have emerged from Wales, the most famous still remain the brothers Anthony of Carmarthenshire. Ivor, Owen and the youngest though best known John Randolph Anthony, each made their Aintree marks over a period exceeding 30 years. It was 23-year-old Ivor who first pitted his skill against the rigours of the National when in 1906 he rode CRAUTACAUN into fourth place behind the Aubrey Hastings-ridden ASCETIC'S SILVER. That same year his youngest brother Jack recorded his first victory over fences and five years later in 1911, when only 21, he acquired his first ride when deputising for the injured Frank Mason on Mr Bibby's GLENSIDE. Having graduated from the somewhat sedate world of show-jumping, through point-to-points to the boisterous all-action activity of steeplechasing, Mr John Randolph Anthony had developed, while still an amateur, a skill and boldness well beyond his years. On the rain-sodden mud that was Aintree racecourse that March day in 1911, Jack Anthony revealed an abundance of those qualities on the one-eyed, broken-winded GLENSIDE, for although left in front when the only other two horses of 26 starters left standing collided with each other, the young Welshman had a very exhausted horse under him and seven awesome fences separating them from victory. Of the only four horses to complete that most gruelling of all Nationals, GLENSIDE was cajoled, nursed and gently guided past the winning post, with the three remote followers all having been remounted.

The following year Jack Anthony was absent from the line-up and it was his big brother Ivor who made the frame for the second time, finishing third on Lord Derby's AXLE PIN behind the brilliant JERRY M. In 1914 it was Owen Anthony's turn to be involved in a Grand National result. Finishing second on IRISH MAIL behind COVERTCOAT, it was to be the only occasion when Owen completed the Grand National course. However, after taking out a trainer's licence in 1921 he prepared MUSIC HALL to win the race in 1922.

Still a member of the unpaid brigade of steeplechase riders, Jack Anthony exhibited his brilliance around Aintree when winning the race again in 1915 with ALLY SLOPER and once more in 1920 aboard the very powerful but wilful TROYTOWN. For the remainder of his riding career Jack Anthony rode as a professional and although another triumph in the National eluded him, before retiring in 1927 he finished second in the race twice with OLD TAY BRIDGE in 1925 and 1926 and in his very last National came third astride BRIGHT'S BOY behind SPRIG and BOVRIL III in 1927. In his second season as a trainer he saddled the favourite EASTER HERO to finish a most unlucky runner-up behind GREGALACH in the 1929 event, the horse having to run the final mile virtually on three legs after spreading a plate. Signing off the Anthony family involvement in the great steeplechase so enriched by their achievements, the brother who began it all, Ivor, trained American-owned KELLSBORO' JACK to win the race in 1933, repeating the process four years later with ROYAL MAIL.

It was from Wales again, this time picturesque Pembrokeshire, that another two brothers briefly, yet positively, flashed with brilliance across the National's rich panoply. Born the sons of a veterinary surgeon, Frederick Brychan Rees, always referred to as Dick, and his elder brother Lewis Bilby each displayed exceptional talent in the

Above: Quickly following on where his brother left off, Lewis Bilby Rees rode MUSIC HALL to a resounding victory in 1922

and finally the Royal Flying Corps. So meteoric was his rise as a brilliant amateur rider after his return to Civvy Street, the demands on his services became so heavy he turned professional after finishing fifth in the 1920 Grand National on NEUROTIC, his first ride in the race. Just a year later, partnering the well fancied SHAUN SPADAH, Dick Rees survived the mayhem of the race to bring his mount home alone the winner, with but three other remounted horses eventually getting round. Despite deciding on a rather early retirement from the saddle, he nonetheless is one of only a handful of riders to have won the big four of jump racing – Grand National, Cheltenham Gold Cup, Champion Hurdle and Grande Steeplechase de Paris. In 1922, just twelve months after his younger brother's triumph, Bilby Rees kept the family name to the fore when giving a perfect example of horsemanship to guide MUSIC HALL to a twelve-length victory. Exactly 40 years later, Bilby's son Bill finished forth in the 1961 Grand National on SCOTTISH FLIGHT II and

saddle, yet it was the younger Dick who won six jockeys' championships between 1920 and 1927. As with many of his generation, Dick's career was delayed through service in the Great War during which he saw action with the Sussex Yeomanry, the Manchester Regiment

Opposite page: Mrs Jenny Pitman with 'Corky', better known as the 1983 winner CORBIERE. Her achievement in becoming the first and as yet only woman to train a National winner came ten years after her ex-husband Richard was narrowly beaten in the race. Her son Mark also came very close to winning it on GARRISON SAVANNAH in 1991

Right: The day the National was 'won by three Furlongs'. REYNOLDSTOWN is led back by owner/trainer Major Noel Furlong after winning the 1935 Grand National in the hands of his son, amateur rider Frank Furlong

although unable to emulate his father and uncle by winning the race, Bill Rees had the distinction of piloting the Queen Mother's THE RIP into seventh place in 1965. In all Bill rode 51 winners for the Queen Mother before severe leg injuries forced him to hang up his boots and in 1973 he became a starter for the Jockey Club.

The headlines of evening newspapers on 29 March 1935, which announced 'Grand National won by three Furlongs', so subtly abbreviated the story of that afternoon's contest at Aintree, with many observers instantly interpreting the words to mean a horse had passed the post almost half a mile ahead of any other. Clever though the pun was, the actual winning distance was three lengths, gained by the eight-year-old almost black REYNOLDSTOWN who was owned, trained and ridden by a person bearing the surname Furlong. Rejected by no less a judge of horseflesh than Mr James V Rank, REYNOLDS TOWN was purchased by Major Noel Furlong, who trained the gelding himself at Skeffington in Leicestershire and duly booked his 25-year-old son Frank to partner it in the National. A subaltern in the 9th Lancers, amateur rider Frank Furlong gave his mount a delightful ride in the race to beat 26 opponents at a starting price of 22/1. REYNOLDSTOWN repeated the victory the following year, on that occasion in the hands of Frank Furlong's brother, officer Fulke Walwyn. With the outbreak of the Second World War, Frank joined the Fleet Air Arm, taking part in the air attack on the German pocket-battleship Bismarck. Lieutenant Commander Francis Furlong, RNVR, lost his life in 1944 when his damaged aircraft crashed on Salisbury Plain.

Another trainer with an extremely talented jockey son was Reg Hobbs, who in 1938 saddled the tiny American-bred stallion BATTLESHIP to run in the Grand National, with his son Bruce in the saddle. In one of the closest finishes ever witnessed in the race, seventeen-year-old Bruce produced a terrific late burst of speed from his mount to catch Irish challenger ROYAL DANIELI on the line and win by a head. Owned by the very wealthy American Mrs Marion du Pont Scott, whose husband was the Hollywood cowboy film star Randolph Scott, BATTLESHIP was instantly retired from racing, returned to the United States and became a great success at stud. After wartime service with the Queen's Own Yorkshire Dragoons, during which he won the Military Cross, Captain Bruce Hobbs became a prominent flat-race trainer based at Palace House, Newmarket.

Ten years after her former husband Richard Pitman came so close to winning the 1973 Grand National on CRISP, Mrs Jenny Pitman became the first woman to train a winner of the race when CORBIERE held on to win by three quarters of a length from Irish representative GREASEPAINT. Quickly becoming one of the leading exponents of her profession, the humorous, down-to-earth Jenny won almost every major

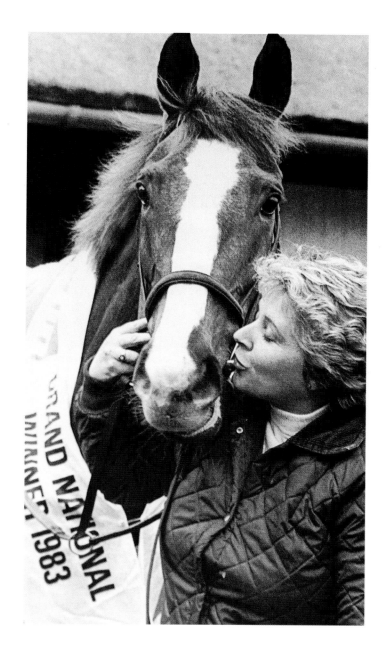

event in National Hunt racing but in 1991 once again suffered the heartbreak Aintree too often brings, when her accomplished eldest son Mark came so close to providing her with a second winner in the race. Riding Cheltenham Gold Cup winner GARRISON SAVANNAH, they had a clear lead with barely 300 yards to run but were caught and beaten close to home by SEAGRAM. With his mother's retirement from the sport in 1999, Mark Pitman took over the mantle of trainer and having already displayed great talent, looks certain to carry on the family tradition with the same passion and dedication.

The 1999 and 2000 Nationals have continued to reveal more of Aintree's 'Family Affairs', revealed in chapter 11.

GRAND NATIONAL
— AINTREE —

MEMORABLE RACES

If one thing can ever be certain about the Grand National, it is that each year the event provides its own special features, the eventual heroes and sufficient talking points to last well into the future.

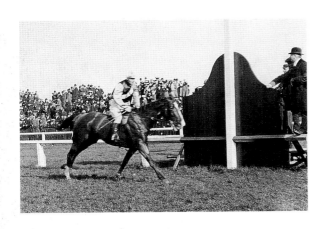

Above: Striding out well to the line, KIRKLAND scores a comfortable three-length victory in the 1905 National

Right: ROUGH QUEST, jumping magnificently, mounts his bid for victory in the latter stages of the 1996 National

From the very beginning, when LOTTERY set the seal on his greatness in winning the first Grand Liverpool Steeplechase, the event attained a reputation for exceptional excitement, drama of the highest degree and a simply inspirational brand of courage. Although by modern standards that chase in 1839 may well be described as inept, it marked the beginning of a sporting contest which would achieve worldwide fame, as well as a regular quantity of controversy.

As the leading steeplechaser of his generation, LOTTERY justified his position as 5/1 favourite with a sparkling display over the ditches, brooks and Wall, producing a winning leap of 30 feet at the final obstacle which amazed all who witnessed it. The be-whiskered Captain Martin Becher also played a major part in that race, without even completing the journey. Riding CONRAD, the Captain was unceremoniously deposited into the first brook and although he never competed in the race again, his name is forever linked with the race in the form of the barrier which bears his name, Becher's Brook.

One of the major factors in the sudden prominence of the Grand Liverpool Steeplechase, as it was known originally, was that it offered the first attractive prize provided for a jumping race. Although frowned on for many years by devotees of flat racing and the governing body of horse racing, the infant sport of steeplechasing was thoroughly popular with the average sportsman, thanks largely to the man still recognised as the 'Father of English Steeplechasing' – Tom Coleman. It appears ironic that just as Coleman's Great St Albans Steeplechase was reaching its demise, fellow inn-keeper William Lynn laid the foundations of an event which would surpass the expectations of all associated with cross-country racing in those early years.

From the very beginning, Aintree's testing contest proved the major annual target of owners, trainers and jockeys, particularly after the race became a handicap in 1843, for the intention of handicapping is to provide every contestant with an equal chance.

If ever an event was designed to stir the imagination, increase the pulse rate and arrest belief, then the great Aintree steeplechase is it. From its earliest

days men and horses have toiled to master this supreme test and through their efforts have emerged stories to challenge the richest imagination. The remarkable no-hopers whose only claim to fame is a National victory; the consistent brave triers repeatedly denied the foremost rewards, and the glorious few who taste the fruits of success more than once.

Always remembering that there is no such thing as a bad Grand National winner, when ageing men of the Turf reach the twilight of their days it is a select band of Aintree heroes which arouse their memories and make them yearn for days long gone. Yet not all can or should be a RED RUM, MANIFESTO or GOLDEN MILLER, for each have encountered and risen above their own adversities in one way or another and all Aintree winners earn their rewards the hard way. With each annual contest a championship for the toughest staying chasers, every race produces a similar pattern for much of the journey but when the pressure is on after the second Becher's, that long run home always tells its own agonising story, the depths of which can only be fully realised by the participants.

VANGUARD 1843

The appointment of Yorkshireman Edward William Topham as Handicapper brought a new stage of development at Aintree. Together with a new title of The Liverpool and National Handicap Steeplechase, it was evident that in the short four years since its inception plans for the future of the race were being judiciously laid.

1843		
1st	VANGUARD	
2nd	NIMROD	**GRAND** ®
3rd	DRAGSMAN	**NATIONAL**
4th	CLAUDE DUVAL	—AINTREE—

That the first Aintree Topham had given much thought to his new position at Liverpool was also clear, for he introduced race cards at Aintree which proved a tremendous help to those attending the event. Less welcome for owners and riders was the re-introduction of the notorious Stone Wall in front of the stands. Dispensed with for the last two years, the Wall came back with the belief that it would provide a more thrilling sight for spectators.

Of the sixteen starters PETER SIMPLE started 3/1 favourite, with the now thirteen-year-old LOTTERY making his fifth appearance in the race at 4/1, and newcomer VANGUARD among the outsiders on the 12/1 mark.

Right: VANGUARD was the first horse to win the race when it became a handicap in 1843. Ridden by the colourful Tom Olliver, VANGUARD provided his jockey with a second successive Grand National victory, Olliver having partnered the 1842 winner GAY LAD. He won the race again in 1853 astride the fifteen-year-old PETER SIMPLE

The property of leading flat-race owner Lord Chesterfield, VANGUARD was of somewhat doubtful parentage, for his sire was said to be either ADVANCE or the well known hunter stallion BELZONI. Nonetheless, the bay gelding's five chase victories before his Aintree attempt earned him eleven stone ten pounds in the handicap and the previous year's successful jockey, Tom Olliver, was sufficiently impressed to accept the ride on him.

A sharp overnight frost rendered the ground hard and left patches of ice in the ditches but from a good start the runners set a decent pace out into the country with only CONSUL failing to survive the first fence. Disputing the lead over the early obstacles, PETER SIMPLE and VICTORIA showed the way to LOTTERY, VANGUARD, TINDERBOX and TEETOTUM with the remainder well in touch. The fall of VICTORIA at the fence before Becher's Brook left VANGUARD in front, with PETER SIMPLE hard on his heels. These two proceeded to dictate the pace over the Brook, around the Canal Turn and back towards the racecourse. Jockey Frisby was suffering a rough ride aboard the erratic PETER SIMPLE, who behaved in his usual unruly manner, though they cleared the Wall just behind the leader VANGUARD, while to their rear the dreaded obstacle claimed both TINDERBOX and TEETOTUM. Both fallen horses lay directly in the path of LOTTERY who, already in mid-flight, produced a spectacular leap reminiscent of that which won him the race four years before, clearing the Wall and both sprawling horses.

Running out of steam after jumping Becher's again, PETER SIMPLE gave way to the

Left: Edward William Topham was known as 'The Wizard' because of his uncanny accuracy at handicapping horse races. Switching from his duties at Chester racecourse, Topham was appointed at Aintree to frame the first handicap on the big race in 1843, a task he performed faultlessly for many years. His descendants controlled the affairs of Liverpool races for the next 130 years

Cheltenham-trained DRAGSMAN who ran on to appear to have the race at his mercy jumping the second last. With an ample advantage over his rivals, DRAGSMAN suddenly swerved away from the final fence, cleared a gate at the side of the course and fully beyond the control of his amateur rider, Mr Crickmere, bolted down a lane. Regaining control of his mount, Crickmere steered the animal back on to the track to finish third behind VANGUARD and NIMROD, beaten a mere three lengths and half a length.

Thus Tom Olliver became the first jockey to win the race in successive years and such was the affection he felt for VANGUARD, when the horse passed away he had a sofa made from its hide.

A mere twelve months later the unfortunate Mr Crickmere himself tasted the joy of success when partnering DISCOUNT to a comfortable National victory.

Left: A delightful sketch of the newly titled Liverpool and National Steeplechase of 1843, showing the leaders at the post and rails following the notorious Stone Wall. The grey PETER SIMPLE is jumping clear, with the famous LOTTERY lying in fifth place in what was to be his final Aintree appearance. It was also the last occasion in which the Wall was used in the race

ABD-EL-KADER
1850 & 1851

When Henry Osborne of County Meath made his return journey from London in 1827, little could he have imagined just how fortuitous his trip would be. Travelling by stage coach, Osborne became impressed with the action of a member of the team pulling the coach - an elegant mare he subsequently purchased for 40 guineas. He named her ENGLISH LASS and succeeded in winning many races with her in Ireland.

1850

1st	ABD-EL-KADER	
2nd	THE KNIGHT OF GWYNNE	GRAND NATIONAL — AINTREE —
3rd	SIR JOHN	
4th	TIPPERARY BOX	

1851

1st	ABD-EL-KADER	
2nd	MARIA DAY	GRAND NATIONAL — AINTREE —
3rd	SIR JOHN	
4th	HALF-AND-HALF	

Less successful at stud, the only foal with any ability born to ENGLISH LASS was a little bay colt given the name ABD-EL-KADER. Affectionately known by all connected with him as 'Little Ab', he developed quickly as a steeplechaser, winning races all over his native land and passing into the ownership of Joe Osborne, the breeder's son, was aimed at the big Liverpool event.

Well known as an authority on breeding, Joe Osborne was a regular contributor to *Bell's Life*, compiled the *Steeplechase Calendar* and despite his literary duties threw his all into training ABD-EL-KADER for Aintree.

With 32 runners composing the largest field yet assembled for a Grand National, 'Little Ab' was overshadowed by the profusion of

Right: ABD-EL-KADER was the son of a mare who at one time had been part of the team which pulled the Shrewsbury mailcoach.

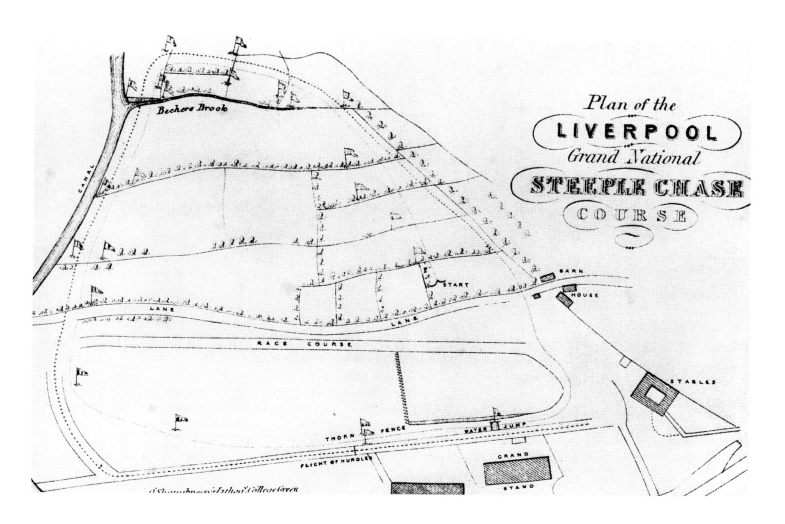

former winners and proven National horses aligned against him, to such an extent that he was totally ignored in the betting. A cracking pace was set straight from the off and little was seen of ABD-EL-KADER during the first circuit as the previous year's first and second, PETER SIMPLE and THE KNIGHT OF GWYNNE, attempted to run the opposition into the ground. Approaching Becher's for the second time, however, jockey Chris Green brought ABD-EL-KADER past horse after horse and, jumping the Brook like a stag, went into a clear lead. Galloping relentlessly, the little bay drew further and further ahead of his rivals as he made his way back towards the packed stands and it was only at the final obstacle that THE KNIGHT OF GWYNNE put in a final desperate challenge. Holding on with tremendous courage, ABD-EL-KADER outstayed his opponent to win by a length, with SIR JOHN

a further three lengths back, third of the seven who completed the course. A double reason to celebrate came for the winning connections when the announcement was made that ABD-EL-KADER had created a new time record for the event; for the first time the race had been run in under ten minutes.

In 1851, as the nation prepared to celebrate the Great Exhibition, 'Little Ab' contested his second National, this time ridden by Irish jockey Terry Abbot and once again he was among the back-markers for most of the first circuit. In another fast-run race, ABD-EL-KADER was foot perfect at every obstacle and once more he bravely held on in a prolonged struggle to win by 'half a neck' from MARIA DAY, with SIR JOHN again third.

As the first horse to win the Grand National not merely twice, but in successive years, the worldwide fame won by ABD-EL-KADER was indeed well and truly earned.

Above: Aintree racecourse in 1848, as documented on a map of that period. One of the earliest of the Grand National course, it clearly shows the area beyond the Melling Lane to be open farmland, with the hedges separating the fields used as obstacles on race days. In most instances the competitors jumped out of one field into another of a lower level

SALAMANDER 1866

Many fine racehorses have been maligned and insulted throughout the history of the Turf but few, if any, before they have even set foot on a racecourse. SALAMANDER aroused the wrath of his breeder Mr Bouchier within hours of the animal being born, simply because the foal was seen to have a crooked foreleg which would obviously have an adverse effect on his value at auction.

1866		
1st	SALAMANDER	
2nd	CORTOLVIN	
3rd	CREOLE	
4th	LIGHTHEART	

GRAND NATIONAL
— AINTREE —

Fortunately the more patient Edward Studd of Rutland bought the horse at a bargain price when the poor creature looked like an 'exhausted scarecrow' and was living in the most dreadful conditions. In due course the deformity corrected itself and SALAMANDER grew into a fine stamp of horse with ability to match his looks.

Although still only a seven-year-old and despite being soundly beaten by 40 lengths at Warwick, the gelding was entered for the 1866 National and veteran amateur Alex Goodman engaged to ride him.

A heavy snow-storm just before the contestants left the paddock failed to dampen the spirits of the vast Aintree crowd and after two false starts the 30

Right: SALAMANDER was rejected by his breeder because as a foal he appeared to have a deformity to one of his forelegs. Having developed into a reliable steeplechaser, he became the property of Edward Studd and won the 1866 Grand National at the generous odds of 40/1

Left: Finch Mason's busy sketch incorporates the connections of victorious SALAMANDER being greeted by the owner Mr Studd, while the inset depicts the popular amateur rider Alex Goodman who guided the winner home. Mr Goodman also won the race on MISS MOWBRAY fourteen years earlier in 1852

runners finally began their journey with ACE OF HEARTS leading them into and over the first fence at a fast gallop. His exuberance got the better of him at the very next obstacle, though, when he swung round at the last moment and in colliding with those behind, created wholesale chaos. From there on riderless horses became more of a problem than usual, the lead changing regularly for the remainder of the first circuit and even at the second Becher's the outcome of the race was uncertain, with the previous year's winner ALCIBIADE falling there when making his bid. Suddenly, to everyone's surprise, SALAMANDER was brought by Alex Goodman from almost last to first, jumping brilliantly and leaving the rest toiling in his wake. Despite a spirited attempt to get on terms by the second favourite CORTOLVIN, SALAMANDER stuck well to his task, running on to beat the challenger by a comfortable ten lengths. Only three others completed what had been a tumultuous race.

For Edward Studd, the man who rescued a horse from the most uncertain of futures, came not just the glory of seeing his faith in SALAMANDER justified in the most arduous race of all, but £40,000 from the betting ring.

His winner started at odds of 40/1. The very next week SALAMANDER proved his Aintree victory was no fluke, romping home in an all-the-way victory in the Warwick Grand Annual Steeplechase. He never ran in the National again but CORTOLVIN, beaten so emphatically at Aintree in 1866, won the race the following year.

Below: Runner-up behind SALAMANDER, CORTOLVIN paid his conqueror a compliment when winning the race himself in 1867

SEAMAN 1882

By the time Lord John Manners of the Grenadier Guards purchased SEAMAN for £2,000, the small though fine-looking gelding was, in the opinion of most Turf pundits, well past any further use for racing. Plagued by sickness from an early age, the Irish-bred gelding had nonetheless won two important long-distance chases in striking fashion in his short career - The Liverpool Hunt Steeplechase at Aintree and The Conyngham Cup at Punchestown.

1882

1st	SEAMAN
2nd	CYRUS
3rd	ZOEDONE

Only three completed the course

GRAND
NATIONAL
— AINTREE —

Placed in the care of Captain James Machell at Newmarket, the famous trainer realised only too well that he had been presented with an almost impossible task. With the Grand National barely four months away, Machell worked ceaselessly in attempting to restore SEAMAN to any semblance of fitness. Of equal concern was the knowledge that the owner, 'Hoppy' Manners, intended partnering the horse at Liverpool. Aware of his trainer's concern at his lack of riding experience, Lord Manners tried to improve the situation by competing in as many amateur events as possible in the time available. Just three weeks before the decisive test in the National, he was rewarded with a victory in Sandown's Grand Military Gold Cup aboard LORD CHANCELLOR.

A heavy fall of snow greeted the twelve runners who made their way to the start on 24 March 1882. Among the excited crowds none was more fearful than Captain James Machell who knew beyond doubt that the diminutive SEAMAN was scarcely three parts fit. For fellow trainer, Irishman Henry Eyre Linde, no such anxiety existed. As the man formerly responsible for the preparation of SEAMAN, Linde was fully aware of the question mark hanging over the readiness of his former charge but naturally his allegiance lay with his own runners, the strongly fancied MOHICAN and CYRUS.

Outsider EAU DE VIE cut out the running straight from the start, jumping boldly and coping well with the heavy going until, at Becher's second time, his rider broke a stirrup leather and the horse veered to the right into the crowd. Left in front now was another long-shot, ZOEDONE, closely followed by the remaining survivors, FAY, CYRUS, SEAMAN and THE SCOT. Back on the racecourse, though, with but two obstacles left, CYRUS struck the front followed by an apparently distressed SEAMAN. A third successive Grand National victory appeared assured for leading Irish amateur Tommy Beasley. Having broken down just before the final hurdle, SEAMAN suddenly rallied with only 300 yards left to run, and to the amazement of all watching, racing virtually on three legs and incredibly brave instinct, got up in the final strides to win by a head. A long way back came the only other finisher, ZOEDONE, to secure third place.

A more than grateful Lord Manners took his champion home to well deserved retirement in which the little bay hero became a much loved pet of his Lordship's children.

FATHER O'FLYNN 1892

In terms of Grand National winners, the final decade of the nineteenth century produced what is usually referred to as 'The Age of the Giants' - a period in which horses with tremendous weight-carrying abilities over the gruelling Aintree course blazed a glory trail which forever after would be a yardstick for equestrian brilliance.

1892		
1st	FATHER O'FLYNN	
2nd	CLOISTER	
3rd	ILEX	
4th	ARDCARN	

GRAND NATIONAL
— AINTREE —

Originator of this accolade was the Irish-bred CLOISTER, whose dam – GRACE II - was so ill-thought of that the village postman rode her to deliver the mail. His story will follow in due course.

Having been beaten by a mere half length on his first National appearance in 1891 when ridden by Captain Roddy Owen, CLOISTER was a most popular 11/2 favourite twelve months later even with the welter burden of twelve stone three pounds. This time round the favourite found a new partner in the form of Mr JC Dormer, while Captain Owen teamed up with Shropshire-bred FATHER O'FLYNN, a 20/1 shot.

With the race run in a thick fog, proceedings out in the country could only be guessed at by spectators in the stands, yet when CLOISTER was seen holding a prominent position over the Water Jump, the cheers rang out. From the second Canal Turn the favourite made the best of his way home, jumping with a breath-taking fluency fast becoming a regular feature of CLOISTER over Liverpool. Only upon returning to the racecourse proper

Left: More of a Hunter Chase specialist than anything else, FATHER O'FLYNN was, in spite of his Irish-sounding name, bred in Shropshire and the rather small gelding was owned by Australian-born Mr Gordon Wilson, a subaltern in the Household Cavalry

did the first threat appear, when FATHER O'FLYNN came full of running to issue a challenge to the favourite. With an advantage in the weights of 26 pounds, FATHER O'FLYNN raced to the front between the final two fences and, staying on with determination, romped home clear of CLOISTER to pass the post fully twenty lengths clear. In third place came the 1890 winner ILEX in front of eight other finishers.

Having achieved his lifelong ambition, Captain Edward Roderic Owen of the Lancashire Fusiliers immediately volunteered for active service with his regiment, serving with distinction in such far-off places as the Gold Coast, Uganda and India. Four years after the day he had most longed for, that Aintree victory which meant so much, Roddy Owen died of cholera during the Dongola Expedition of 1896 and was buried far from the scene of his most momentous victory. His name appears not only on Aintree's golden Roll of Honour but is also honoured by the Owen Falls in Kenya being named after this very gallant gentleman.

Far left: Edward Roderic Owen was born in 1856 at Bettws in Montgomeryshire and after being educated at Eton, served as an officer with the 20th East Devonshire Regiment. Returning to England after ten years duty in Canada, Cyprus, Malta and India, Captain Own rode 254 winners over the sticks, culminating in his Grand national victory in 1892 on FATHER O'FLYNN

KIRKLAND 1905

Bred in County Limerick by the Reverend Clifford, KIRKLAND was purchased at an early age by Mr Frank Bibby, the Liverpool industrialist, and quickly repaid that gentleman by winning eight times over fences before the age of seven. Most significantly, the last of those victories was gained in the prestigious Grand Sefton Steeplechase at Aintree, where he beat that great Liverpool specialist MANIFESTO by eight lengths.

1905

1st	KIRKLAND
2nd	NAPPER TANDY
3rd	BUCKAWAY II
4th	RANUNCULUS

GRAND NATIONAL
— AINTREE —

Even though KIRKLAND received two and half stone from the dual National winner that day in November 1902, it was a splendid achievement for such a young horse and proved that he could certainly survive those daunting fences. Without a win to his name over the next two years, however, many believed that it was a case of too much too soon for KIRKLAND and some critics suggested the gelding had been over-raced in his formative years. Whatever the truth, there could be no denying he knew his way around Aintree, for he finished a creditable fourth behind DRUMCREE in the 1903 Grand National, and twelve months later was runner-up in the race to the New Zealand-bred winner MOIFAA.

Impressed with KIRKLAND's Aintree deeds to date, his connections laid out plans for an all-out effort in the 1905 National and after a bloodless victory over a single opponent at Ludlow in February, his preparation was geared to just one other event: the Aintree spectacular on the last day in March.

Mr Lort Phillips, who owned a share in the horse, trained KIRKLAND at Lawrenny Park, near

Tenby in Pembrokeshire, although the licence was held by a Mr Thomas. Such was the enthusiasm of both Frank Bibby and Mr Phillips, they paid jockey Frank Mason £300 not to ride in any races for two weeks before the big event for fear an injury would deprive them of the valuable assistance the Liverpool-born rider would provide.

The previous year's winner, MOIFAA, this time carrying the colours of His Majesty King Edward VII, started 4/1 favourite with KIRKLAND, second in the market at 6/1, obviously a popular choice of the locals with both owner and jockey Liverpool men. All 27 runners cleared the first fence safely but falls came thick and fast from the second onwards and at the halfway stage the well strung out field were led over the Water by

riderless ASCETIC'S SILVER. When MOIFAA crashed at the second Becher's, RANUNCULUS led from TIMOTHY TITUS, NAPPER TANDY and the steadily improving KIRKLAND. The fence after Valentine's Brook put paid to the chances of TIMOTHY TITUS and after jumping two more fences, Frank Bibby made his move. Crossing Melling Road at the Anchor Bridge, KIRKLAND raced into the lead with only the loose ASCETIC'S SILVER ahead of him. Jumping the final two obstacles cleanly, he galloped on to win by three lengths from NAPPER TANDY, with BUCKAWAY II third and RANUNCULUS fourth.

Having gained his greatest victory, KIRKLAND rarely raced again, although in 1908 he started favourite for the National, only to finish seventh after being remounted.

Above: Liverpool-owned and ridden, KIRKLAND became the only Welsh trained National winner in 1905 when beating 26 rivals as the 6/1 second favourite

Far left: Six times champion steeplechase jockey Frank Mason became the only Liverpool-born professional to win the race when piloting KIRKLAND in 1905 for owner Mr Frank Bibby, the Liverpool industrialist. The popular jockey was known on the racecourse as 'Tich' Mason

SPRIG 1927

The Grand National of 1927 produced one of the most thrilling finishes in years and with it, moments of poignancy rarely witnessed on a racecourse. Ten years earlier, whilst home on leave from Flanders during the Great War, Captain Richard Partridge of the Shropshire Yeomanry bred a chestnut colt which he named SPRIG. Hoping that when peace was restored he would one day partner the horse in the Grand National, the Captain returned to duty at the front where he was tragically killed in action shortly before the armistice.

1927	
1st	SPRIG
2nd	BOVRIL III
3rd	BRIGHT'S BOY
4th	DRINMOND

GRAND NATIONAL
— AINTREE —

Aware of her son's deepest wish, Mrs Mary Partridge resolved to put SPRIG into training with the dream that, if good enough, she may at least accomplish a part of Richard's Aintree ambition. Sent to trainer Tom Leader at Newmarket, the gelding grew into a strong, impressive looking jumper, although he was by no means the easiest animal to train and was prone to leg problems.

Early in his career, SPRIG won the valuable Victory Hurdle at Manchester and two years later, in 1924, proved equally adept over the larger obstacles when successful in the Stanley Chase at Liverpool. In the run-up to the 1925 Grand National, SPRIG ran four times without

Above: Jockey Thomas Edward Leader, always referred to as Ted, provided SPRIG with the ideal partner in 1927, while also making the success a father and son affair. Leader junior was the son of Tom Leader who trained the horse

catching the judge's eye and as a result was readily available at 33/1 for the National. With a most impressive performance in his debut over the maximum Aintree distance, SPRIG was well up with the leaders at the second Canal Turn and after meeting with much interference, from that point stayed on gamely to finish a far from disgraced fourth behind the winner DOUBLE CHANCE.

It was a similar story the following year with Mrs Partridge's gelding 5/1 favourite this time and again giving a flawless display of jumping to finish once more in fourth place to the rear of American-owned JACK HORNER.

Recognised now as a genuine Liverpool horse, SPRIG shot up in the handicap for the 1927 National, yet both trainer Tom Leader and his jockey son Ted who rode the horse, were confident that barring accidents this must surely be their year. Fourth in the weights with twelve stone four pounds, SPRIG once more started favourite at 8/1, largely on the basis of winning the Select Handicap Chase at Sandown just eight days before his important Aintree engagement.

On heavy going totally against those at the top of the handicap, the 37 runners dashed away across Melling Road into the mist. Only when they came back on to the racecourse towards the end of the first circuit could it be seen that the field was greatly reduced in number. Among the leaders was SPRIG and at Becher's second time he was a close-up sixth, behind BOVRIL III, DWARF OF THE FOREST, KEEP COOL, MASTER BILLIE and BRIGHT'S BOY. At the Canal Turn, though, he put in such an enormous leap that he landed in front. With BRIGHT'S BOY challenging strongly all the way on to the final fence, it was clear that SPRIG still had plenty to do. Landing in front over the last, SPRIG set sail for home some lengths ahead of the remainder, but suddenly the 100/1 outsider BOVRIL III came with a blistering run, drawing closer to the favourite with every stride. At the post SPRIG held on for a length victory, with BRIGHT'S BOY a further length behind BOVRIL III in third place. At the third attempt, gallant SPRIG provided the late Captain Partridge with the memorial he would most have wished for.

Below: The 8/1 favourite SPRIG gets a late shock as the 100/1 outsider BOVRIL III delivers a last minute challenge to get within a length of victory in 1927. BRIGHT'S BOY, ridden by Jack Anthony, is a close-up third

BOGSKAR 1940

Seven months after the commencement of the Second World War, the curtain fell on Aintree's famous steeplechase with what was to be the last running of the race for six years. Virtually everyone attending the racecourse was attired in uniforms of various branches of the armed forces from all over the British Empire, and with this including owners, trainers and jockeys, the scene in the parade ring before the big race resembled a gathering for a military tatoo.

1940		
1st	BOGSKAR	
2nd	MACMOFFAT	GRAND NATIONAL
3rd	GOLD ARROW	— AINTREE —
4th	SYMAETHIS	

Favourite of the 30 runners was Irish challenger ROYAL DANIELI at 4/1, who two years before was denied National victory by the narrowest margin in the final strides by the pride of America, BATTLESHIP. Runner-up twelve months before, MACMOFFAT figured prominently in the betting, as also did Miss Dorothy Paget's KILSTAR, the Danny Morgan-ridden MILANO and George Owen's mount THE PROFESSOR II.

Despite having won the National Trial Steeplechase at Gatwick, BOGSKAR, who was owned and trained by Lord Stalbridge at Eastbury in Berkshire, was readily available at 25/1 in the betting. Booked to ride the horse at Aintree was Welsh-born jockey Mervyn Jones, a flight-sergeant in

Top right: The 25/1 winner BOGSKAR was owned and trained by Lord Stalbridge, a member of the Jockey Club, and won what was to be the last Grand National for six years because of the Second World War

Right: BOGSKAR wins the 1940 Grand National by four lengths from Scottish-trained MACMOFFAT. The riderless NATIONAL NIGHT passes the post in front after having unseated his jockey Hywel Anthony Jones at the halfway stage of the race

the Royal Air Force who had to seek permission to compete in the race from his air-commodore. Upon being informed by Jones that he had recently passed his navigation examination, his superior officer instructed him to 'Go and navigate BOGSKAR around Aintree then, and if you don't, we'll put you through another navigation exam'.

With favourite ROYAL DANIELI setting a hot pace up front on the first circuit, falls were few and far between and MACMOFFAT led over the Water Jump closely followed by ROYAL DANIELI, GOLD ARROW and VENTURESOME KNIGHT. In this order they swept over Becher's Brook for the final time, where BOGSKAR began to close on the leaders. But with Valentine's safely behind them, MACMOFFAT opened up a promising lead, with his nearest companion the riderless NATIONAL NIGHT.

When ROYAL DANIELI fell at the penultimate fence, MACMOFFAT appeared to have the race at his mercy, though as he came to the last BOGSKAR was brought alongside him with a well timed challenge by Mervyn Jones. Recovering from a slight mistake on landing, BOGSKAR produced the better turn of foot to race home the winner by four lengths, although the loose horse NATIONAL NIGHT actually passed the post first. Strange to relate, NATIONAL NIGHT had started the journey with Hywel Jones, brother of the winning rider, in the saddle but they parted company at the fourteenth.

As the throngs left Aintree to a far from certain future, there could be no telling when, if ever, they would meet again. Of the many who made the supreme sacrifice was Flight-sergeant Mervyn Anthony Jones, lost in action at the age of 22.

ALDANITI 1981

It is doubtful if one single incident in the long history of the Grand National has aroused such admiration and sense of well-being as that generated by ALDANITI and Bob Champion at Aintree in 1981. So well documented has been this story since that incredible victory against all the odds, that hardly anyone can be unaware of its significance. Yet so inspirational was the success of cancer-stricken jockey Bob Champion and leg-weary ALDANITI in the toughest steeplechase on earth, they became National heroes in the truest sense.

1981

1st	ALDANITI	
2nd	SPARTAN MISSILE	
3rd	ROYAL MAIL	
4th	THREE TO ONE	

GRAND NATIONAL
— AINTREE —

Far right: Becher's Brook in 1981, with the eventual winner ALDANITI jumping like a stag. Leading for most of the way, ALDANITI and his jockey Bob Champion scored a National success which led to probably the most emotional scenes ever witnessed at any sporting event

Right: With the eyes of the world's media firmly fixed upon them, Bob Champion and ALDANITI face their adoring public the day after their date with destiny at the Findon stables of trainer Josh Gifford

Barely four months after partnering ALDANITI into third place in the 1979 Cheltenham Gold Cup, Bob Champion was given the devastating news that he was suffering from cancer and that without the most austere course of chemotherapy treatment, his life expectancy could be measured in months. Through endless months of torturous hospitalisation, he pursued an impossible aim to reinforce his battered spirit. That one single vision stood like a beacon of hope for the distressed Champion, a hopeless wish to somehow, some way, partner ALDANITI in the Grand National.

His regular visitors while in hospital, Nick Embiricos and Josh Gifford, respectively owner and trainer of ALDANITI, listened sympathetically to their

jockey without once mentioning that the horse was presenting them with serious problems concerning its future. Always a victim of leg trouble, ALDANITI had just broken down yet again and with the animal's future looking as dismal as Bob Champion's, all they could do was humour the jockey and his dreams of Aintree glory.

Mercifully, the owner's devoted lady groom, Beryl Millam, nursed the stricken ALDANITI back to a semblance of fitness, sufficient enough to allow a still recovering Bob Champion to take the horse out on to the Aintree turf for their date with destiny on 4 April 1981.

Either despite or because of the tribulations the gallant pair had endured, ALDANITI went off 10/1 second favourite of the 39 contestants, with the proven Liverpool performer SPARTAN MISSILE best fancied at 8/1. Here, too, lay another nostalgic facet of Grand National folklore: 54-year-old John Thorne bred, owned, trained and rode SPARTAN MISSILE in an attempt to fulfil his life-long ambition by winning the National.

From a good start they charged across the Melling Road towards the first fence, at which ALDANITI landed on his nose after a mistake. But his jockey sat tight and together they continued in the hunt, albeit at the rear of the field. By the time they came back to the racecourse, though, ALDANITI had made up the lost ground to dispute the lead over the Chair with SEBASTIAN V, ROYAL STUART and ZONGALERO. Dictating affairs by several lengths, ALDANITI jumped Becher's in fantastic style, while a long way back SPARTAN MISSILE seemed to be labouring after a blunder at the eighteenth. Three from home, ALDANITI made an error which allowed ROYAL MAIL to come into a challenging position, but when the latter misjudged the second last, the cheers began ringing out for the brave ALDANITI and Champion. Resisting the powerful late run of SPARTAN MISSILE, ALDANITI held on for a four-length victory. With such generous sportsmanship, the first to congratulate Bob Champion after passing the post was John Thorne, rider of the runner-up. Eleven months later Thorne was killed in a point-to-point.

ROUGH QUEST 1996

By the time the fifth Martell-sponsored Grand National was run in 1996, concern was expressed that not since the French company's first involvement with the event in 1992 had a full complement of 40 competitors taken part. A gradual reduction of horses taking part began when two less than the maximum 40 permitted faced the starter for the race declared void in 1993. Twelve months later, only 36 took part and in 1995 the trend continued when 35 made the bid for Aintree glory.

1996		
1st	ROUGH QUEST	
2nd	ENCORE UN PEU	GRAND NATIONAL — AINTREE —
3rd	SUPERIOR FINISH	
4th	SIR PETER LELY	

Worst of all in recent times, however, came with just 27 contestants in 1996, the smallest number to compete in the National since 1960. For many chasing enthusiasts, the situation seemed ominous.

Admittedly, it could be said that what the race lacked in quantity was more than made up for by quality, yet still sceptics questioned why owners seemed less interested in competing in the great chase.

Runner-up in the recent Cheltenham Gold Cup, ROUGH QUEST found most favour with punters, being installed 7/1 favourite from such other worthies as YOUNG HUSTLER, SON OF WAR, LIFE OF A LORD, SUPERIOR FINISH and PARTY POLITICS.

Standing in for the regular starter was Gerry Scott, winning jockey in 1960 on MERRYMAN II, who thus became the only man to both ride a National winner and officiate as starter for the race. From a perfect start YOUNG HUSTLER, SURE METAL and THREE BROWNIES made the early running. Jumping the Canal Turn, SURE METAL was giving Donald McCain junior the ride of his life at the head of the field. By the time they reached the Chair, THREE BROWNIES had gained a narrow lead over YOUNG HUSTLER, SURE METAL, GREENHILL RAFFLES and SUPERIOR FINISH. On the run back to Becher's Brook, Mick Fitzgerald took ROUGH QUEST smoothly down the outside of the track to within striking distance of the leaders. Also making steady progress at this point was ENCORE UN PEU, who upon returning to the racecourse with two fences remaining, swept into what looked an unassailable lead.

Landing five lengths clear on the flat and with every obstacle safely behind him, David Bridgwater drove ENCORE UN PEU on towards what looked to be a comfortable triumph and that coveted place in the record books. But behind and between the ears of ROUGH QUEST, Mick Fitzgerald glimpsed the briefest semblance of a chance to turn defeat into victory and with one final sublime effort flashed past his opponent to win by a length and a half.

Back in the winner's enclosure, Mick Fitzgerald's ecstasy turned to agony with the announcement that the stewards had called for an enquiry and it took fully fifteen minutes more before the connections of ROUGH QUEST were allowed to celebrate in the time honoured fashion, when the decision was given that the result should stand.

When questioned by the BBC's Desmond Lynam concerning what winning the National felt like, the winning jockey declared: 'After that, sex is an anti-climax'.

Left: The perfect partnership in action, ROUGH QUEST and jockey Mick Fitzgerald on their way to the post. Winning the race at his second attempt, having fallen at the first fence in 1995 with TINRYLAND, Fitzgerald rode a beautifully judged race to bring ROUGH QUEST with a well-timed challenge to overtake the leader after passing the elbow

Far left: Mr Terry Casey, trainer of ROUGH QUEST, who won the National twelve years after his first attempt with HAZY DAWN in 1984. One of the nicest men in racing, Terry saddled ROUGH QUEST to run a creditable second in the 1996 Cheltenham Gold Cup. Discovering the horse was suffering with a muscle enzyme disorder, he worked a minor miracle in turning him into a National winner just weeks later

8

GRAND NATIONAL
—AINTREE—

GREAT HORSES

There may well be improbable winners of the National and there have certainly been those who have benefited from a giant-sized piece of luck, but by general consent there is no such thing as a bad Grand National winner.

Above: In preparation for yet another tilt at the National, 'Rummy' completely at home on his Southport Beach gallops

Right: LORD GYLLENE, ridden by Tony Dobbin, takes the Water Jump en route to victory in 1997

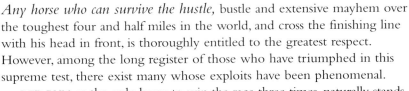

Any horse who can survive the hustle, bustle and extensive mayhem over the toughest four and half miles in the world, and cross the finishing line with his head in front, is thoroughly entitled to the greatest respect. However, among the long register of those who have triumphed in this supreme test, there exist many whose exploits have been phenomenal.

RED RUM, as the only horse to win the race three times, naturally stands supreme as the ultimate in courageous endeavour: no praise can ever be too high for such a unique character. But there are many others among Aintree's bravest of the brave whose exploits are worthy of distinct admiration.

Setting a trail of greatness, LOTTERY began it all in 1839 as the outstanding steeplechaser of the age, his triumph as favourite in the first big Aintree challenge setting a seal on his prowess.

PETER SIMPLE became the second horse to score a double victory in the race, although his second success came two years after ABD-EL-KADER repeated his win in 1851. Both THE LAMB and THE COLONEL demonstrated their excellent ability also as dual winners and the magnificent MANIFESTO at the turn of the century emerged as possibly the most robust and consistent of all. From eight starts in the race he won twice, was third three times, fourth once and only once failed to complete the course he knew so well.

CLOISTER, JERRY M and POETHLYN each triumphantly carried the maximum burden of twelve stone seven pounds to success, and the brilliant, if enigmatic, GOLDEN MILLER totally deserved his title of 'Horse of the Century'.

In more recent times FREEBOOTER, MERRYMAN II, CORBIERE and WEST TIP have all captured that special position in the annals of Aintree folklore. Such is the essence of this annual pursuit for National glory, one can look forward to a future which will bring forth horses whose deeds will excite, thrill and inspire in the manner displayed by every Aintree hero of the past.

THE LAMB 1868 & 1871

It has often been claimed that Grand National winners come in all shapes, sizes and colours, and perhaps one of the earliest examples of this was a little horse named THE LAMB. *Bred by a Mr Henchy in County Limerick, from his earliest days the tiny grey colt bore not the slightest resemblance to a future racehorse, his weedy appearance and meek nature leading to the breeder's young son naming him* THE LAMB.

GRAND NATIONAL
— AINTREE —

RACE RECORD

1868	Winner
1871	Winner
1872	4th

Henchy junior, a delicate boy who suffered much illness, treated the horse as a pet until the child's premature death led to THE LAMB being sold for £30. To the surprise of everyone who knew the horse, he began winning small flat races and with maturity and such a gentle nature, became very reliable in the hunting field. Offered for sale to Mr Edward Studd, whose SALAMANDER won the Grand National in 1866, THE LAMB was rejected out of hand with the scornful remark that 'The animal is not fit to carry a man's boots'. Like many before and since, Mr Studd would live to regret his rash decision.

An impressive victory in the Kildare Hunt Plate at Punchestown brought the grey to the attention of Lord Poulett, an English nobleman determined to one day win the National, a race he came close to winning when his CORTOLVIN was runner-up to SALAMANDER. Purchasing THE LAMB in the

Right: After winning the 1868 National, the tiny grey THE LAMB suffered from a wasting disease which threatened to bring a premature end to his racing career. Three years later, however, he made a successful return to Aintree to fulfil the dream of his owner Lord Poulett by scoring a second victory in the 1871 race

autumn of 1867, His Lordship at once booked his close friend, the highly talented amateur rider George Ede, to ride the horse in the next Grand National. In his usual manner Ede rode at Aintree under the assumed name of 'Mr Edwards'.

Standing barely fifteen and a half hands high, it was suggested by many Aintree observers that THE LAMB would not be able to see over the fences let alone jump them, but by the end of the 1868 National Mr Studd was not alone in having to eat his words. Given a copybook ride by his partner, THE LAMB kept the leaders well in his sights the whole way, jumped superbly throughout and in a driving finish held on impressively to win by two lengths from PEARL DIVER, with previous winner ALCIBIADE taking third place.

After just two outings the following season, tragedy struck THE LAMB and his connections when the grey was stricken with a dreadful wasting disease which at one point threatened the animal's life and kept him away from racing for two years. During that period George Ede had sadly been killed in a steeplechase fall and in attempting to find a replacement rider, Lord Poulett wrote the following words to another brilliant amateur Thomas Pickernell, fully four months before the 1871 Grand National.

Left: One of the original thirteen men responsible for founding the National Hunt Committee in 1866, the 6th Earl Lord Poulett was a constant supporter of steeplechasing from the earliest days of the sport and a regular visitor to Aintree racecourse

My Dear Tommy,

Let me know for certain if you can ride for me at Liverpool on THE LAMB. I dreamt twice last night I saw the race run. The first dream he was last and finished among the carriages. The second dream, I should think an hour afterwards, I saw the Liverpool run. He won by four lengths and you rode him and I stood close to the winning post at the turn. I saw the cerise and blue sleeves and you, as plain as I write this. Now let me know as soon as you can and say nothing to anyone.

Yours sincerely,
Poulett

That was one dream which did indeed become reality. On 21 March 1871, the Grand National was won by THE LAMB two lengths ahead of DESPATCH, with SCARRINGTON four lengths away, third of the 25 runners.

Left: George Matthew Ede, better known to racegoers as 'Mr Edwards', was one of the finest amateur riders of his day as well as being an accomplished cricketer. Together with his friend and patron Lord Poulett, he founded the Hampshire Cricket Club and in 1863 scored 1,200 runs. He died three days after receiving injuries in a fall in the Sefton Chase at Aintree in 1870

THE COLONEL 1869 & 1870

It is very rare for two dual Grand National winners to be foaled within twelve months of each other; for each to be entire horses at the time of their greatest triumphs, it is even more unusual. Yet within twelve months of THE LAMB reserving his place on Aintree's Roll of Honour after his first success when just six years old, along came THE COLONEL at the same age to carve his own chapter into racing history.

GRAND NATIONAL
— AINTREE —

RACE RECORD	
1869	Winner
1870	Winner
1871	6th

Right: Bred and owned by Mr John Weyman in Shropshire, the almost black entire THE COLONEL won the Grand National in both 1869 and 1870, ridden on both occasions by the incomparable George Stevens. After finishing sixth under top weight of twelve stone eight pounds in the 1871 race, he was sent to Germany to become the charger of Kaiser Wilhelm I

Bred by John Weyman at Brampton in Shropshire, THE COLONEL was by the stallion KNIGHT OF KARS, who inherited strong blood from his Exmoor pony ancestors. A prolific winner of hurdle races in the colours of his breeder, THE COLONEL was competing in only his second steeplechase when lining up with 21 others for the start of the 1869 Grand National.

Piloted by the peerless George Stevens, a jockey already with three National wins to his credit, the horse was ridden in the familiar manner of his rider – hunting round in the rear for the first circuit before making a late challenging run. As in the past the tactics worked perfectly, with THE COLONEL moving smoothly through the field to join the leaders after Becher's second time round. Taking up the running three from home, Stevens and THE COLONEL raced on to win comfortably by three lengths from HALL COURT.

Despite being raised nineteen pounds in the handicap and without the benefit of a run since winning the National, THE COLONEL went off 7/2 favourite to reproduce his Aintree victory in 1870. Again ridden by George Stevens, he justified the support to get the better of THE DOCTOR by a neck in a desperately close finish.

Subsequently sold to the German owner Baron Oppenheim, in whose colours he finished sixth behind THE LAMB in 1871, THE COLONEL eventually became a successful stallion at stud in Beberbeck and as a part-time occupation, served as the charger of Emperor Wilhelm I for ceremonial occasions.

Jockey George Stevens was unfortunately killed in a riding accident near his home in Cheltenham merely three months after partnering THE COLONEL at Aintree in 1871. His total of five winning rides in the Grand National remains a record to this day.

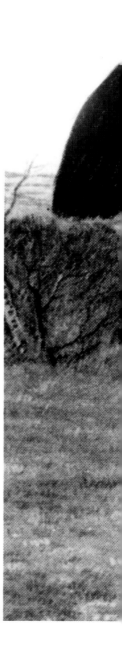

GAMECOCK 1887

One of many amazing characteristics of the Grand National is the number of horses who, in spite of the severity of the course, regularly appear to rise above themselves when competing at Aintree. A perfect example of this was the bay gelding GAMECOCK, who between the years 1885 and 1891 figured prominently in the big race on no fewer than seven occasions.

GRAND NATIONAL
— AINTREE —

RACE RECORD

1885	Did not finish
1886	3rd
1887	Winner
1888	7th
1889	10th
1890	Did not finish
1891	6th

Right: The very tough and consistent GAMECOCK, who in seven seasons as a jumper won no less than 28 steeplechases including the 1887 Grand National. The gelding also finished third, sixth, seventh and tenth in the race

Trained by James Gordon near Tarporley in Cheshire and owned by 'Mr E Jay', in truth Liverpool businessman Mr Thornewill, GAMECOCK was an out-and-out stayer in addition to being a jumper good enough to hold his own with the best. The winner of 28 steeplechases through a very busy and distinguished career, GAMECOCK frequently competed at Aintree where he became a great favourite of local racegoers.

Running in his first National in 1885, while still only a six-year-old, the gelding failed to get round, but twelve months later he finished a creditable third behind OLD JOE and TOO GOOD. As if to prove this effort had taken nothing out of him, a fortnight later he won the four mile Grand International Steeplechase at Sandown Park.

The following season GAMECOCK made Aintree his exclusive stamping ground in no uncertain terms. Finishing a promising third in Liverpool's Grand Sefton Chase on 10 November 1886, he came out the following day to run former National winner ROQUEFORT to a length in the Hapsburg Chase over the same fences. His final race before making a third attempt at Aintree's supreme test came three weeks later when going under by only a neck in the Great Sandown Chase. In the remaining three months until Aintree, he was kept in peak condition with daily four-mile gallops at Oulton Park.

Grand National day on 25 March 1887 dawned bright and clear, with good going which suited all sixteen

runners. Favourite at 9/2 was Irish-trained SPAHI, a brilliant performer on the flat, though he had never run in either a hurdle race or steeplechase. Seemingly unimpressed with GAMECOCK's experience over this course, most punters ignored him in the betting, allowing his starting price to be a generous 20/1. Jumping off handily, GAMECOCK stayed well in touch for most of the journey, lying a close-up seventh over the Water, by which time it was known that the favourite had fallen early on. After ROQUEFORT ran out

turning for home, the race looked at the mercy of SAVOYARD who cleared the last with a slight advantage, but GAMECOCK gained the upper hand close to home to win by three lengths. Obviously none the worse for his exertions, the gelding raced over the course 24 hours later to win the Champion Chase very easily.

A competitor in each of the next four Nationals, GAMECOCK completed the course every year except when falling in 1890

CLOISTER 1893

Not since before 1843, when the race became a handicap, had a horse carried the huge burden of twelve stone to victory in the blue riband of steeplechasing. Through the years many had tried, some had come agonisingly close and too many had been denied National glory solely through conceding too much weight to inferior opponents.

GRAND NATIONAL
— AINTREE —

RACE RECORD	
1891	2nd
1892	2nd
1893	Winner

Right: Mr Arthur Yates, whose great-uncle John Elmore owned LOTTERY, was an outstanding amateur rider who rode over 460 winners before turning his talents to training. In his new capacity Yates sent out almost 3,000 winners from his establishment at Bishop's Sutton in Hampshire, among them the brilliant if frustrating CLOISTER and the 1885 National winner ROQUEFORT

Far right: Irish-bred CLOISTER became the first horse to carry twelve stone seven pounds to victory in the race in 1893 after finishing second in both the previous Nationals. The gelding's future career was shrouded in mystery and suggestions that bookmakers were in some way involved with the late withdrawal of the horse from the race in both 1894 and 1895

Early in the final decade of the nineteenth century, however, there arrived at Aintree a horse destined not just to beat that elusive 'weight barrier', but one who was to set a standard by which all future National winners would be measured. Fathered by ASCETIC, the outstanding jumping stallion of his era, CLOISTER was from the mare GRACE II, an animal considered so moderate that the village postman was allowed to deliver the mail astride her. Developing rapidly into a horse of great substance, CLOISTER evidently inherited his sire's outstanding qualities for while still only four years old he won three times over fences, including the Irish Grand Military Chase at Punchestown and, more significantly, the Aintree Hunt Steeplechase over the Grand National fences.

Purchased by Lord Dudley, the son of ASCETIC was prepared for the 1891 Liverpool spectacular by Richard Marsh. After running a superb race, he was only beaten by half a length in a stirring finish by COME AWAY. After such an impressive performance CLOISTER was bought by Mr Charles Duff, transferred to the stables of Arthur Yates and was sent again to Liverpool to run in the 1892 Grand National. Presenting a delightful display of fencing under twelve stone three pounds, CLOISTER looked an assured winner. But with only two fences left to jump, he was overtaken by FATHER O'FLYNN, to whom he was conceding 26 pounds. CLOISTER finished second for the second successive year.

A far less active campaign was agreed upon for a third tilt at the National, CLOISTER having only one outing before the big race and that was the Grand Sefton Steeplechase over three miles of Aintree's demanding country. Making every yard of the running under top weight of twelve stone seven pounds, CLOISTER won in what was described by racecourse officials as 'a common canter'. Next stop was the Grand National itself, over four months ahead on 24 March 1893.

The 9/2 favourite of fifteen runners, again heading the handicap with twelve stone seven pounds and with his usual partner Bill Dollery in the saddle, CLOISTER made a virtual procession of the race. Four lengths to the good over the Water Jump, still at the head of affairs rounding the Canal Turn for the second time and well clear jumping the last fence, CLOISTER romped home the easiest winner of the race ever seen. A huge 40 lengths behind the winner came AESOP, with a future National winner WHY NOT a distance back in third place. All present that day freely agreed they had witnessed a wonder horse demolishing his rivals.

Sadly the future of CLOISTER was clouded in mystery, suspicion and rumours of blatant chicanery, which unfairly cast a shadow over the horse and his connections. In both years following his majestic victory, the horse was withdrawn under dubious circumstances just days before each Grand National after being a roaring favourite for months. Worse yet, the bookmaking fraternity apparently had prior knowledge of the favourite's scratching from the race. A most regrettable footnote to the career of a brave and brilliant horse.

MANIFESTO 1897 & 1899

Having waited 50 years to see a steeplechaser who could earn the accolade of greatness by defying the handicapper in the toughest equine contest on earth, the racing public soon encountered another worthy of the highest respect.

GRAND NATIONAL
— AINTREE —

RACE RECORD

1895	4th
1896	Did not finish
1897	Winner
1899	Winner
1900	3rd
1902	3rd
1903	3rd
1904	8th

MANIFESTO *was bred by Mr Harry Dyas* in County Meath and born in 1888 from a mating between MAN OF WAR and VAE VICTIS. Although generally described as 'raw-boned and rather plain in appearance', he made a promising introduction to racing when trotting up in a Maiden Hurdle event at Manchester in 1892. Two months later while still just four years old, MANIFESTO gave a foretaste of future fame, carrying off the Irish Champion Steeplechase at Leopardstown. Three years later his first attempt in the National produced a workmanlike performance as he finished fourth behind fellow Irish challenger WILD MAN FROM BORNEO. But in the 1896 race his effort was short lived when another horse collided with him at the first fence.

Favourite of 28 runners at 6/1 in 1897, MANIFESTO gave a brilliant exhibition of jumping from start to finish, romping home twenty lengths clear of his nearest rival FILBERT. It was a stunning victory for his owner/breeder Harry Dyas, who having taken a small fortune from the bookies was persuaded to sell MANIFESTO the following year to Mr John Bulteel for £4,000.

Left: In the immortal words of Austrian artist Emil Adam: 'Mein Gott! Zis is a racehorse'. Ian Carter's superb impression of the great MANIFESTO after his second victory in 1899

Withdrawn from the race through injury in 1898, MANIFESTO returned to Aintree for the last National of the nineteenth century with top weight of twelve stone seven pounds, carrying a new jockey, George Williamson, in Mr Bulteel's light blue and cherry colours. Conserving his mount's energy under such a massive burden, George Williamson prudently kept clear of trouble on the first circuit and only when the runners approached Becher's again could MANIFESTO be seen to be making ground from the rear. Three fences from home he struck the front, leaving the rest toiling in his wake. Clearing the final two fences as fluently as all before, he passed the post five lengths in front of the nearest pursuer FORD OF FYNE.

Such now was his reputation, in 1900 the handicapper asked the impossible of the dual National winner, allocating him twelve stone thirteen pounds. It was surely this which prevented MANIFESTO winning a well deserved third victory in the race. Approaching the last fence in front, he was overtaken by the Royal competitor AMBUSH II at the last, yet bravely stayed on to finish third four lengths and a neck behind AMBUSH II and BARSAC respectively.

Third again in both 1902 and 1903, MANIFESTO by this time was considered an Aintree institution. When going out for the final time in the 1904 Grand National, he received rapturous applause from the grateful crowds. Courageous to the very end, the sixteen-year-old MANIFESTO finished eighth of the 26 runners at the conclusion of a thirteen-season career which included a record eight appearances in the Grand National.

Left: An unusual photograph of MANIFESTO jumping the preliminary hurdle before the start of the 1899 race. The practice of warming up before the National by jumping this hurdle was dispensed with in 1908

GOLDEN MILLER 1934

If any race has ever regularly made thoroughbred experts look fools, than the Grand National is surely it, for through the years many winners of this event have been the product of unknown and humble parentage. A classic case in point is the horse who by the middle of the 1930s had unanimously and affectionately become known as 'The Horse of the Century'.

GRAND NATIONAL
— AINTREE —

RACE RECORD

1933	Did not finish
1934	Winner
1935	Did not finish
1936	Did not finish
1937	Did not finish

GOLDEN MILLER was bred in County Meath by Laurence Geraghty and was by the stallion GOLDCOURT out of a mare named MILLER'S PRIDE. Never having appeared on a racecourse, the sire was considered by many unfit for stud duties, which was reflected in the fee for his services – a meagre five guineas. The nearest the dam came to success on the turf was to finish second in a steeplechase worth just £22 at Pilltown in Ireland. Sold as a yearling for 120 guineas to farmer Paddy Quinn of Tipperary, GOLDEN MILLER remained unbroken for a further two years until spotted in one of Quinn's fields by Captain Farmer, a Leicestershire horse-dealer. Purchased by him for 500 guineas on behalf of the Suffolk trainer Basil Briscoe, the unraced gelding crossed the Irish Sea to England to begin a meteoric rise to international fame.

A most unenthusiastic beginner, his sluggishness brought the comment from Briscoe's head-lad, Sam Tidy, that 'GOLDEN MILLER was a damned good name for a damn bad horse'.

nought. Cutting the sharp angle too acutely, he unseated his rider and left KELLSBORO' JACK to go on and win.

On the most perfect of spring days, GOLDEN MILLER, again with twelve stone two pounds, lined up second favourite at 8/1 for the 1934 National, only seventeen days after scoring a hat-trick of Cheltenham Gold Cup wins. Kept to the rear by jockey Gerry Wilson for most of the first round, GOLDEN MILLER moved into fourth place jumping the Water and back in the country was in contention for the remainder of the journey. Drawing level with the leader DELANEIGE at the last fence, GOLDEN MILLER sprinted away on the flat for a five-length victory. To increase cause for celebration, it was announced he had set a new time record for the race.

In each of his next three attempts to repeat a National victory, 'The Horse of the Century' failed to complete the course, giving rise to the belief that he had taken a dislike to Aintree. Whatever the truth may be, GOLDEN MILLER remains the only horse to win the Cheltenham Gold Cup and Grand National in the same year.

Left: Seven times champion jockey Gerry Wilson partnered the famous GOLDEN MILLER to two Gold Cup victories and that memorable Aintree success of 1934. As a trainer he saddled the 1945 Champion Hurdle winner BRAINS TRUST before becoming the licensee of the Marquis of Granby Hotel near Newbury

Far left: Five lengths clear of his nearest rival, GOLDEN MILLER sets a new time record for the race, which was to last until the victory of RED RUM in 1973

Below: GOLDEN MILLER with his owner the Honourable Dorothy Paget, the daughter of Lord Queenborough

As if hearing and taking exception to the remark, GOLDEN MILLER suddenly and to everyone's surprise found new interest and vigour in racing and began winning contests. In due course he became the property of the Honourable Miss Dorothy Paget and it was her colours he carried for the remainder of his illustrious career.

In 1932 he won his first Cheltenham Gold Cup, something he was to make rather a habit of doing, for he went on to win the race for the next four years. Still only a six-year-old, GOLDEN MILLER was allocated twelve stone two pounds for his first tilt at the Grand National, but such was his reputation he was made 9/1 favourite of the 34 runners. With few casualties on the first circuit, the favourite was in a handy position going back into the country, coping well with the unusual fences and beginning to make ground on the leaders. Surviving a slight error at Becher's Brook, GOLDEN MILLER moved into second place at the next and appeared to be still full of running, but the very next obstacle, the Canal Turn, brought his labours to

FREEBOOTER 1950

Born in the early years of the Second World War, when horse racing was the furthest thing from most people's minds, FREEBOOTER revived memories of the great jumping heroes of the past in those austere years after hostilities ceased.

GRAND NATIONAL
— AINTREE —

RACE RECORD

1950	Winner
1951	Did not finish
1952	Did not finish

Bred in County Waterford by William Phelan, the son of STEEL POINT developed into an extremely strong, perfect example of a thoroughbred, and his elegant conformation quickly attracted the attention of Irish trainer Dan Moore. Purchased by the former jockey for 620 guineas, FREEBOOTER took well to racing, winning two bumper races in his native land before being sold to Mrs Lurline Brotherton for 3,000 guineas and entering the yard of Yorkshire trainer Bobby Renton.

The epitome of that elusive breed, 'a genuine Liverpool horse', FREEBOOTER excelled over Aintree's demanding obstacles. After winning both the Champion and Grand Sefton Chases there in 1949, he was recognised as a serious prospect for the 1950 Grand National. Teaming up with the gelding for the big event was 26-year-old Jimmy Power, coincidentally also born in Waterford. They attracted sufficient support to start 10/1 joint-favourites with the previous year's runner-up ROIMOND.

Away to a good start, the 49 runners sped away into the country at a fast pace with MONAVEEN showing the way over Becher's from FREEBOOTER, ROIMOND, INCHMORE and STOCKMAN, but the strong gallop led to many falling by the wayside. Still among the leaders approaching the Chair in front of the stands, FREEBOOTER met the obstacle all wrong, striking it heavily with his chest. Making an incredible recovery from a mistake which would have turned most horses over, FREEBOOTER scrambled on with Jimmy Power precariously hanging on to his mount's neck as he laboured to get back in the saddle. Considerately allowing the horse time to recover, the jockey made up lost ground on the run back to Becher's, where with a brilliant leap FREEBOOTER moved into third place. From the second Canal Turn the race developed into a duel between FREEBOOTER and the more experienced CLONCARRIG, with first one then the other getting his head in front. Well clear of the rest of the field returning to the racecourse, they remained alongside each other until CLONCARRIG clipped the top of the penultimate fence and toppled to the ground. FREEBOOTER jumped the last two fences cleanly, romping away to win unchallenged, fifteen lengths clear of the six other survivors.

Top weight with twelve stone seven pounds the following year, FREEBOOTER was a victim of the bad start which led to twelve horses coming to grief at the first fence. Only NICKEL COIN and ROYAL TAN got round without falling. In 1952, once more with twelve stone seven pounds, the great Aintree specialist was travelling well just behind the leader at the second Canal Turn when he crumpled on

landing, leaving TEAL with the simplest of tasks to continue on to victory.

He never ran in the race again, but in November 1953, with jockey George Slack deputising for the injured Jimmy Power, FREEBOOTER smoothly made a procession of the Becher Chase at Aintree to win as he pleased. Upon unsaddling the old horse, his jockey informed the questioning press that he'd 'just been given a most enjoyable conducted tour of Aintree'.

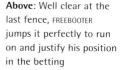

Above: Well clear at the last fence, FREEBOOTER jumps it perfectly to run on and justify his position in the betting

Far left: One of the finest photographs ever taken of Becher's Brook, giving a perfect impression of the tremendous drop on the landing side. Joint-favourite FREEBOOTER is seen landing in the lead first time round in 1950, from the Royal challenger MONAVEEN, who finished fifth

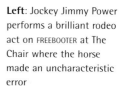

Left: Jockey Jimmy Power performs a brilliant rodeo act on FREEBOOTER at The Chair where the horse made an uncharacteristic error

RED RUM 1973, 1974 & 1977

Seldom, if ever, have the deeds of a steeplechase racehorse aroused the imagination, lifted the spirits, or invoked such admiration of so many millions as did those of the unforgettable RED RUM. By any standards, in any number of ways, this was a horse genuinely unique.

GRAND NATIONAL

— AINTREE —

RACE RECORD

1973	Winner
1974	Winner
1975	2nd
1976	2nd
1977	Winner

As if ordained by fate, he arrived on the National glory trail from the most unlikely background at a time when the very future of the Grand National hung in the balance. In five magical years of Aintree endeavour, RED RUM inspired a whole generation into questioning if the world could afford to lose one of its most valuable sporting institutions. Such was the manner of his phenomenal success, it leaves little elaboration from a humble admirer to portray the story of such a brilliant equine athlete whose achievements speak so profoundly for themselves.

Curiously, yet fittingly, RED RUM made his very first appearance on a racecourse at Aintree the day before the 1967 Grand National: the contest, the most humble of two-year-old selling plates over a straight five furlongs. Few who witnessed RED RUM battling his heart out that afternoon, to get up and force a dead-heat with CURLICUE, could ever have dreamed they were watching a horse who within a decade would totally rewrite the Grand National record books.

Far right: An unprecedented third win in racing's toughest test is manfully earned by everyone's favourite racehorse RED RUM. The man sharing this record-breaking achievement is Tommy Stack who earlier in the horse's career had been his trainer

Right: En route to his second successive Grand National triumph, RED RUM makes light of his twelve stone top weight with a spectacular leap at Becher's second time around in 1974

By 1973 RED RUM had many miles on the clock, having competed for numerous owners and trainers on the flat, over hurdles and in the most demanding of all activities, steeplechasing. On 31 March that year he lined up with 37 others at the start of the Grand National, joint favourite at 9/1 with the Australian champion CRISP. Having made almost the entire running, CRISP led over the final fence fully fifteen lengths ahead of the locally trained RED RUM. With a courageous determination which was to become his trademark, RED RUM clawed back victory from defeat yard by punishing yard, to win in the very last strides by three quarters of a length.

A little of the gloss was taken off his brave performance when the media, in sympathy with the runner-up, pointed out that RED RUM was in receipt of 23 pounds from CRISP. Twelve months on, that criticism was totally laid to rest, RED RUM giving a peerless exhibition of jumping under top weight of twelve stone, to beat dual Gold Cup winner

L'ESCARGOT by a comfortable seven lengths. In both 1975 and 1976 'Rummy' was glorious in defeat, runner-up on both occasions under top weight, but on that April day in 1977 when new meaning was given to the words sheer brilliance, he rewarded everyone privileged to be present with the most scintillating piece of Turf history-making. Romping home 25 lengths clear to become the only horse ever to win the Grand National three times, he more than justified his euphoric trainer Donald McCain's description of the achievement as 'bloody marvellous'.

In May 1995 Aintree Racecourse laid on a special 30th birthday celebration for the 'King of Aintree', with the guest of honour himself completely at ease among his adoring fans. Five months later RED RUM died and was buried alongside the winning post he so often graced at Aintree.

No final resting place could have been more appropriate, for RED RUM typified so completely the spirit of the place and the race.

GRITTAR 1982

After many years of continuing uncertainty concerning Aintree and the Grand National's future,

the Aintree Grand National Appeal was set up by the Jockey Club with the intention of raising enough funds to

purchase the racecourse and ensure its future.

GRAND NATIONAL
— AINTREE —

RACE RECORD

1982	Winner
1983	5th
1984	10th

With the richest prize yet on offer for the race – £52,507 to the winner – the 1982 renewal attracted a very competitive assembly of horses but far and away the most popular choice among the betting community was the hunter-chaser GRITTAR. Bred by his owner Frank Gilman of Morcott, Leicestershire, the nine-year-old had progressed from flat racing, through hurdling, to become one of the most reliable staying chasers in the land.

Trained by owner-breeder Gilman, GRITTAR was a superb jumper endowed with boundless stamina. In 1981 he reached the peak of hunter-chasing success when winning both the Cheltenham and Liverpool Foxhunter Chases. Taking a most ambitious course, Frank Gilman set his sights on the extreme jumping test, the Liverpool Grand National on 3 April 1982, and most daringly decided a stab at the Cheltenham Gold Cup en route.

Giving a more than good account of himself at Prestbury Park, the nine-year-old finished a promising sixth behind that most consistent of jumpers SILVER BUCK in the Gold Cup. So impressive was his effort, he was immediately installed favourite for the National.

Right: Celebrating the success of GRITTAR the day after the race, owner-breeder Frank Gilman and Dick Saunders have every reason to feel happy

Left: At 48 years of age, Northamptonshire farmer Dick Saunders becomes the oldest rider ever to win the National, with the 7/1 favourite and former winner of the Liverpool Foxhunters' Steeplechase — GRITTAR — carrying him to a comfortable victory

Partnered by veteran amateur rider, 48-year-old Northamptonshire farmer Dick Saunders, GRITTAR was sent off the 7/1 favourite and fortunately avoided the trouble at the first fence where the field of 39 was reduced by ten, with 1981's winner ALDANITI among the fallers. Riding a most judicious race, Dick Saunders kept GRITTAR well in sight of the leading group. Over the Water at the halfway stage they lay in a comfortable fifth place. A mistake by SAINT FILLANS at the second Becher's allowed GRITTAR to gain the lead and from there on only a fall could alter the eventual result. Making the best of his way home with clean jumping at every obstacle, GRITTAR quickly asserted himself and despite a solitary mistake at the final fence, galloped on to a fifteen-length victory over HARD OUTLOOK and the remounted LOVING WORDS. The first favourite to succeed in the race for 22 years, GRITTAR was a most popular winner and amidst the celebrations in the unsaddling ring, winning rider Dick Saunders at once announced his retirement from the saddle. It was his first and only ride in the National and as the only member of the Jockey Club to pilot home a National winner, he was warmly congratulated the following week by his peers at Portman Square.

LORD GYLLENE 1997

Just moments before the start of the 1997 National, the cruellest, most callous and cowardly telephone warning was received at the racecourse, to the effect that an explosive device had been installed at Aintree. That the desired chaos was avoided is a credit to the racecourse authorities, whose evacuation of the site was executed with clockwork precision. If fear, discomfort and a sense of helplessness were the desired effect of those responsible, then yes, perhaps their objective was achieved.

GRAND NATIONAL

— AINTREE —

RACE RECORD

| 1997 | Winner |

But in reality, the following 48 hours became a conquest for decency, tolerance and the finest elements of humanity, with the citizens of Liverpool responding most generously in caring for and accommodating countless numbers of stranded racegoers.

The mammoth task of searching and securing the area completed, horses and spectators returned for the re-scheduled 150th running of the Grand National late on Monday afternoon, 7 April 1997. Of the 36 runners, GO BALLISTIC started 7/1 favourite. To a mighty roar from the still anxious crowds, the race got under way at one minute past five o'clock.

Prominent from the very first fence, the New Zealand-bred LORD GYLLENE proceeded to set a brisk pace, closely followed by SUNY BAY, SMITH'S BAND, NORTHERN HIDE and NAHTHEN LAD. Returning to the racecourse near the end of the first circuit, it was pleasing to see that few were missing from those who set off. With CELTIC ABBEY the only casualty at the Chair, they raced on to the Water Jump. With LORD GYLLENE and SMITH'S BAND matching strides in front, the riderless GLEMOT suddenly and dangerously sprinted

between the two, then cut to the left across LORD GYLLENE just as the leader approached the obstacle. Only the razor-sharp reflexes of jockey Tony Dobbin prevented a collision as he astutely manoeuvered his mount away from the intruder to steer LORD GYLLENE safely over the Water Jump. From that point on the New Zealand horse was never headed, galloping on close to the inside rail and jumping splendidly the whole way. SUNY BAY improved his position over the Canal Turn, looking poised to challenge but a mistake at

the final open ditch put paid to his chances. LORD GYLLENE raced on to win by 25 lengths from SUNY BAY, CAMELOT KNIGHT and BUCKBOARD BOUNCE.

It was a tremendous triumph for all connected with the winner - Stan Clarke, the owner; Steve Brookshaw, the trainer; and especially the ice-cool jockey Tony Dobbin.

More than that, though, it was an overwhelming success for all who endured with humour, stoicism and dignity Aintree's 'long weekend'.

Above: Better late than never. The postponed 1997 Grand National takes place 48 hours later than expected but LORD GYLLENE makes the long wait worthwhile with a resounding performance

Far left: New Zealand-bred LORD GYLLENE wins the 1997 National by 25 lengths at 14/1 in the hands of jockey Tony Dobbin

9

GRAND NATIONAL
— AINTREE —

Above: Thomas Pickernell, known on the racecourse as 'Mr Thomas', began as a pupil of Tom Olliver. His excellent riding in Tasmania led to the jockeys there signing a petition to curtail his activities in their homeland

Right: Twenty-year-old Brian Fletcher is led in after winning the 1968 Grand National on RED ALLIGATOR. It was his second ride in the race, having finished third on the same horse in the chaotic 1967 event

GREAT JOCKEYS

As with LOTTERY in 1839, the initial display of supreme jockeyship witnessed at Aintree came from that first winner's partner in victory, Jem Mason, known affectionately as 'Dandy Jem'. The principal cross-country rider of his day, Mason was blessed with a natural style in the saddle, said to be 'copied by many, but bettered by none'.

Hot on his heels in the early days of chasing came 'Black Tom' Olliver, a close friend as well as rival of Jem Mason's and a man whose adventures in private life were as colourful as his exploits on the Turf. A competitor in the National for the better part of two decades, Olliver became the first to ride three winners of the race.

Without question the most successful man to pit his ability against the demands of Aintree was Cheltenham-born George Stevens who, in a lifetime cut short through a tragically ludicrous accident, partnered no less than five Grand National winners.

In an age teeming with outstanding horsemen of the highest possible calibre, nineteenth century Aintree was also graced with the presence of such outstanding riders as John Maunsell Richardson, Tommy Pickernell, Ted Wilson, Tom and Harry Beasley and the incomparable Arthur Nightingall.

All but the last competed as amateurs, while others among the paid ranks to excel themselves on Aintree's proving ground of greatness include such larger than life characters as Percy Woodland, Frank Mason, Ernie Piggott and the immaculate Welsh wizard of the saddle, Frederick Brychan Rees.

In more recent times such notables as Arthur Thompson, Bryan Marshall, Michael Scudamore and the maestro himself, the fabulous Fred Winter, extended the realm of their predecessors to levels of excellence undreamt of.

The seemingly endless abundance of riding skill exhibited at Aintree from generation to generation for more than 160 years is as apparent today as ever before and admired throughout the world.

Raised to the present rare level of excellence by such dedicated practitioners of their art as Richard Dunwoody, Carl Llewellyn, Mick Fitzgerald, Brendan Powell and Paul Carberry, the feats of Jem Mason, Tom Olliver and all who have known the ecstasy of Grand National success, have been paid their highest tribute.

Tom Olliver

One of the wittiest, most generous and likeable characters in the early days of steeplechasing, Tom Olliver was as brilliant a horseman as he was careless in affairs concerning money and women.

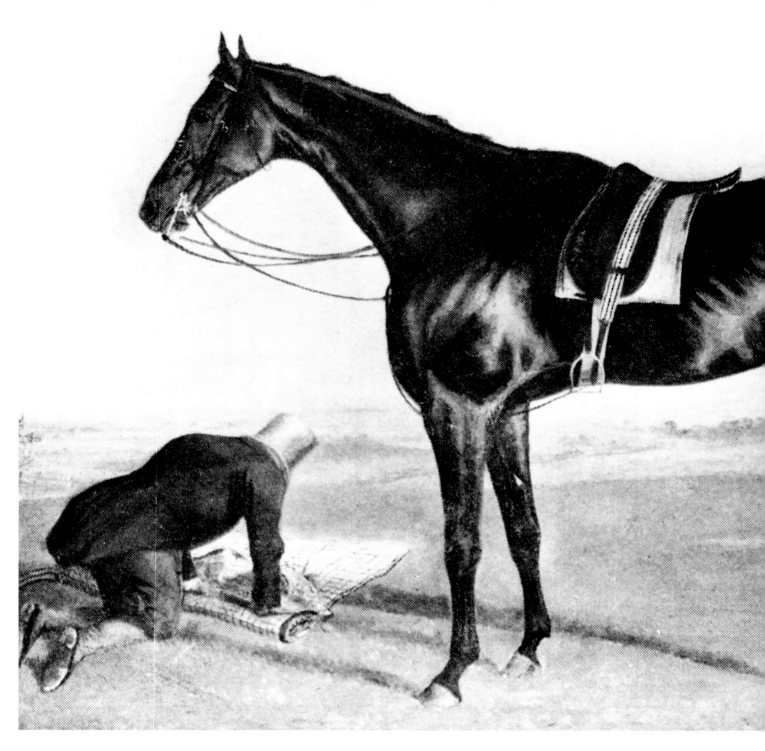

Born in Sussex into a family of sixteen children, his childhood was impoverished but from his earliest years Tom was a genius when it came to horses. Fearless in the extreme, young Olliver could master the most fractious animal in seconds with a gentle hand and a few kindly words. With a dark complexion and thick black hair, a legacy of his Spanish-gypsy ancestors which earned him the name 'Black Tom', he quickly earned a reputation as a brave and talented cross-country rider, becoming the confidante of such as Captain Martin Becher, Tom Coleman and close friend Jem Mason.

Beaten into second place behind Mason and LOTTERY in 1839 when aboard SEVENTY FOUR, Tom Olliver quickly put the Aintree record straight by winning the Grand Liverpool Steeplechase on GAY LAD in 1842 and again the following year with VANGUARD, when the race became a handicap and the Liverpool and National Chase. Eleven years later, in 1853, Tom Olliver became the first man to score a hat-trick of winning rides in the race when partnering the fifteen-year-old PETER SIMPLE to a comfortable three-length victory.

Despite, or perhaps because of his brilliance in the saddle, 'Black Tom' was rarely out of debt and lost many winning rides because of incarceration behind the walls of a debtor's prison, where his frequent visitors consisted of cavalry officer friends to whom he was tutor in the art of race-riding. When asked by one of the officers during a period inside if there was anything he required, Tom Olliver at once replied: 'Send me a damned good wall jumper'.

As a coach for up-and-coming riders, Tom Olliver was as talented as he was astride a horse, among those he taught being such notable Aintree winners as Tommy Pickernell, George Stevens, William Archer and 'Josie' Little. It was Captain Little who in 1848 rode his own CHANDLER to get up in the closing stages of the National and beat Tom Olliver on THE CURATE into second place.

After all these years of Aintree history, 'Black Tom' remains the man to have taken part in the most Grand Nationals, eighteen in all. Apart from winning the race three times, he also finished second three times and once third in a career ended in 1859 when he retired from the saddle.

After taking the role of landlord at The Star in Leamington for a number of years, Olliver moved to Wroughton where he trained horses with much success and, in fact, prepared GEORGE FREDERICK for the Epsom Derby of 1874. Sadly Olliver did not live to see the colt's Derby victory, for he died shortly before the race.

Typical of the man, who retained his wit to the very end, shortly before his death he was asked by a troublesome owner what the staying potential was of his animal. The horse in question was particularly slow and without hesitation Olliver replied: 'Honoured Sir, your horse can stay four miles but takes a damned long time to do it'.

Left: After coming second on SEVENTY FOUR behind LOTTERY in 1839, the devil-may-care Tom Olliver quickly became established as one of the finest cross-country riders in the land. His first winner of Aintree's big steeplechase was GAY LAD (pictured) in 1842, owned by Mr John Elmore, the owner of LOTTERY

George Stevens

Born near Cheltenham in 1833, George Stevens ran away from home as a boy to work in a racing stable,

benefiting from the tutelage of the great Tom Olliver. Though frail and sickly, weighing in fact less than nine stone,

Stevens learned his trade well from the master.

Right: George Stevens was born near Cheltenham and as a boy was coached in the art of race riding by Tom Olliver. Before his untimely death when only 38, he rode the winner of the National a record five times

Below: George Stevens rode his first Grand National winner on FREETRADER in 1856 at the age of 23

His first encounter with the Grand National came at the age of nineteen when he made his debut in the race of 1852 on board the 100/1 shot ROYAL BLUE. Among the fallen that day, four years later he partnered FREETRADER in the race for owner Mr W Barnett, a man from his home town of Cheltenham, who also had the better fancied SIR PETER LAURIE representing him. Riding what was to become his hallmark at Aintree – a waiting race – George Stevens produced FREETRADER perfectly to challenge two others at the final fence. In a tight finish, he won by half a length from MINERVA and MINOS.

His second visit to Aintree's winner's enclosure came in 1863 after riding Lord Coventry's mare EMBLEM to a twenty-length victory, producing another perfect display of jockeyship over the huge fences. Such was the affection the jockey felt for EMBLEM, he named

his cottage at Cleeve Hill, Cheltenham, after the mare. When she was sidelined through injury before the 1864 National, Stevens had no hesitation in choosing her full sister EMBLEMATIC as his mount in the race. Also owned by Lord Coventry, EMBLEMATIC was a weedy looking individual, with spindly legs. On looks alone, she was thought by the experts to have no chance at all. They reckoned, of course, without the genius of Stevens. Getting his mount back in the race after she stumbled at the Water Jump, the Cheltenham jockey made ground hand-over-fist second time round and after jumping clear at the last, out-ran the previous year's runner-up ARBURY for a three-length victory. Favourite to repeat the win the following year, EMBLEMATIC and Stevens finished a creditable third behind two very good horses, ALCIBIADE and HALL COURT, the winning rider – Captain Coventry – ironically being a cousin of Lord Coventry, the owner of EMBLEM and EMBLEMATIC.

Having secured his second and third victories in the race with mares, George Stevens created an unbeatable sequence of wins with an almost black entire horse, THE COLONEL. Riding the six-year-old in 1869, he turned the tables on ALCIBIADE and HALL COURT, behind whom Stevens had finished third four years before, bringing THE COLONEL home three lengths clear. In 1870 it was a much closer affair, but again the wizardry of Stevens prevailed and THE COLONEL held on to win by a neck and provide his jockey with a fifth Grand National victory.

Amid speculation of his impending retirement, George Stevens competed in his last National in 1871, once more on THE COLONEL, and finished sixth of the 25 runners behind THE LAMB. Scarcely three months later came the tragic news that George Stevens, one of the greatest jump jockeys of all time and certainly a master of his trade when it came to the Grand National, had been killed. Far from the dangers he faced each day on the racecourse, he had been thrown from his hack while enjoying a leisurely ride back to his home on Cleeve Hill. Striking his head against a boulder, he died from his injuries.

Below: The mare EMBLEM, who provided George Stevens with his second success in the race and after whom the jockey named his cottage on Cleeve Hill, Cheltenham. Twelve months after this victory, Stevens rode EMBLEM's full sister EMBLEMATIC to glory to keep the National prize well and truly in the family

Thomas Pickernell

Known throughout his lengthy riding career as 'Mr Thomas', Tommy Pickernell, like many others from distinguished families, employed the pseudonym at a time when steeplechasing was still frowned upon by certain sections of society.

Born at Witley in Worcestershire in 1834, he was educated at Cheltenham College where he became a close friend of fellow pupil Adam Lindsay Gordon. In his spare time he extended his lessons to include learning to ride under the guidance of Tom Olliver.

Probably as a result of Tommy's increasing interest in equestrianism, upon leaving college his family packed him off to Tasmania to learn sheep farming, but even after a tedious sea voyage his heart remained set on riding horses. It was in that far-off land that he rode his first winner and such was his subsequent success, the local professionals all signed a petition requesting him to curtail his activities. Returning to

England, 'Mr Thomas' soon established himself as one of the leading jump riders in the country, at a period when there was an abundance of extremely talented horsemen.

He won the Grand National for the first time in 1860 on ANATIS, with whom he had finished fifth the previous year when having his initial ride in the race. In winning with the 7/2 favourite, 'Mr Thomas' ignored the offer of a £1,000 bribe aimed at him near the finish of the race by the rider of second placed HUNTSMAN.

In constant demand by owners, Tommy competed a further eight times in the National over the next ten years with only a third place to show for his efforts. But early in 1871, he

Below: After finishing fifth on ANATIS in the 1859 race, Pickernell rode the mare to victory the following year when she started 7/2 favourite and beat 19 opponents

Above: PATHFINDER and 'Mr Thomas' on the way to victory in 1875, four years after the rider's second success in the race aboard the dream horse THE LAMB

received the famous letter from Lord Poulett concerning His Lordship's dreams about a grey entire called THE LAMB. Riding a perfectly judged race on the little grey, as well as extricating his mount from a predicament at the Canal Turn, Pickernell brought the horse home two lengths clear to score his second National success and receive a tremendous ovation from the crowds. Re-establishing his partnership with THE LAMB the following year, the pair finished a fourteen-length fourth behind the winner CASSE TETE, under the massive burden for such a little horse of twelve stone seven pounds.

Still riding with a skill and flair which were the envy of many half his age, Tommy took the mount in the Aintree epic of 1875 on a little-known eight-year-old Epsom-trained gelding called PATHFINDER. Now 41 years old, the veteran horseman was in the habit of taking a little liquid fortifier before a race and on this occasion presumably took one swallow too

many, for when taking his place at the start, found it necessary to ask another jockey which way he should be facing. On very heavy going the runners encountered many problems out in the country and less than half of those who started were still in the contest over the Water Jump. So sluggish did PATHFINDER feel as they neared Becher's again, his jockey was on the point of calling it a day and pulling him up. It was only to give the owners a run for their money that Pickernell continued. After jumping Valentine's, however, he was surprised to find PATHFINDER running on with renewed vigour and jumping the last in contention with the mare DAINTY, raced on to win by half a length.

After breaking his jaw in three places and losing an eye in an horrific fall at Sandown in 1877, Tommy Pickernell hung up his boots to become the first National Hunt Inspector of Courses. Upon retirement he went to live in Kings Heath, Birmingham, where he died in 1912.

Above: PATHFINDER and 'Mr Thomas' on the way to victory in 1875, four years after the rider's second success in the race aboard the dream horse THE LAMB

Arthur Nightingall

It was little wonder that Arthur Nightingall rose to be one of the most dedicated and respected jockeys of the nineteenth century, for he was born in 1868 into the famous Epsom racing family, and his father John owned and trained SHIFNAL to win the 1878 Grand National.

Making his first National appearance in 1886 when riding THE BADGER, eighteen-year-old Arthur acquitted himself well in bringing the 25/1 chance home a respectable fifth behind the winner OLD JOE. Two years later he piloted the same horse into ninth place in the race.

Making the frame for the first time in the premier steeplechase in 1889, Arthur Nightingall guided the gelding M.P. around to collect third place prize-money. By this time he had met up with a young horse called ILEX who was to become a great favourite of the jockey and his entire family.

Initially unimpressed with the animal when engaged to ride it at Leicester, considering it to be 'a shaggy looking beast with no front, a large belly and equipped with four dubious looking bandages', Arthur Nightingall rapidly changed his mind – ILEX gave him a most delightful ride coming home a long way in front of the opposition. Subsequently bought by George Masterman and trained by Arthur's father John, the lightly raced chestnut was specially prepared for the 1890 Grand National in which he started 4/1 favourite and naturally was ridden by Arthur. Giving a superb exhibition of jumping over the mighty fences, ILEX ran out the easiest of winners by twelve lengths. Just eight days later he crowned a memorable year for all concerned by winning the valuable Lancashire Chase at Manchester. Third in the race in both 1891 and 1892 with Arthur in the saddle, ILEX confirmed

Right: The second of Nightingall's three big Aintree winners, WHY NOT competed in the National seven times and apart from his success in 1894, completed the course in all but one of his other attempts

himself a genuine Liverpool horse, but after his final game effort in 1892, broke down so badly he was retired from racing. In praise of the horse who proved him wrong, Arthur Nightingall very positively declared: 'ILEX was absolutely the best horse I ever rode'.

For the third year in succession, he had to be content with the minor honours at Aintree the following year when third again, this time with the ageing bay gelding WHY NOT. Like a fine wine, though, WHY NOT apparently improved with age, for in 1894 – at the advanced age of thirteen – he provided Arthur Nightingall with a second National success.

It was unanimously agreed by all at Aintree on 29 March 1901 that, as a result of the atrocious weather conditions, the afternoon's Grand National should be either postponed or

abandoned. After a brief consultation, however, the stewards decided to go ahead with the race in the midst of a raging blizzard. Fortunately and with tremendous foresight, trainer Bernard Bletsoe took the precaution with his horse GRUDON of spreading two pounds of butter into its hooves and together with the distinct advantage of Arthur Nightingall upon his back, GRUDON 'skated home' by four lengths. As intended, the application of butter to GRUDON's feet prevented snow from balling in his hooves.

After his final National ride in 1904, Arthur hung up his boots. Following in the footsteps of his father he became a fine trainer, with horses belonging to the Prince of Wales and Lord Marcus Beresford entrusted to his care. He passed away peacefully in 1944.

Above: Considered the best professional jockey of his era, Arthur Nightingall was a member of the famous Epsom racing family and this his first National winner – ILEX – was trained by his father John Nightingall

Jack Anthony

One of only three amateur riders to win the jockeys' championship in the twentieth century, Jack Anthony was also one of just two to win the Grand National three times during that period.

Above: The youngest of three brothers who each made major contributions to jump racing, John Randoph Anthony won the National three times before turning professional, on GLENSIDE in 1911, ALLY SLOPER in 1915 and the powerful TROYTOWN in 1920

Right: The twelve-length winner of the 1920 National TROYTOWN, with Jack Anthony in the saddle

Born the youngest of three sons in Carmarthenshire in 1890, like his brothers he began riding at a very early age, rapidly making his mark as a veritable natural in the show-jumping ring and in point-to-points. Racing under Rules as an amateur, Jack rode his first winner in 1906 and five years later secured his first mount in the Grand National on Frank Bibby's GLENSIDE, a faller in the previous year's race.

Considered by many less than an ideal conveyance for an amateur's first tilt at the National, the nine-year-old gelding had only one eye, was broken-winded and regarded as not a genuine character. With torrential rain turning the course into a quagmire, falls were plentiful from the very first fence. Going back into the country for the final time, only a handful were left in the race, with GLENSIDE well to the rear. The fancied CAUBEEN and RATHNALLY led over Becher's but at the next fence collided with each other when making for a hole in the obstacle. Suddenly and unbelievably GLENSIDE was left in front. With all the others having fallen, Jack Anthony nursed his mount back over Valentine's and the big ditch beyond, he and his horse a lonely team with but the occasional loose horse for company on the long haul home. GLENSIDE appeared very distressed with two left to jump and it was only the skill and sympathy of his rider which pulled him through to win a taxing contest by twenty lengths from RATHNALLY, SHADY GIRL and FOOL-HARDY, each of whom had been remounted.

Three years after this momentous victory Jack Anthony topped the winning jockeys' list with 60 winners and in 1915 rode the six-year-old ALLY SLOPER to Aintree glory, creating another piece of National history in the process

– the owner of ALLY SLOPER being Lady Nelson, the first woman to lead in a Grand National winner.

On another day of non-stop rain, 26 March 1920, Mr Anthony faced the Liverpool starter on 6/1 second favourite TROYTOWN, trained by the Royal winning jockey of twenty years earlier Algernon Anthony (no relation of the Welsh Anthonys). Making every yard of the running and virtually pulling his rider's arms from their sockets, the powerhouse of a horse

romped to a most convincing twelve-length victory, despite almost taking the 26th fence by the roots. In Jack Anthony's words, 'The hardest part of the race was stopping him going round a third time'.

Turning professional in 1921, Jack Anthony was champion jockey again the following year and in the final three years of his jockeyship came agonisingly close to breaking George Steven's record of five National wins. Landing first over the last fence in 1925 and 1926 on OLD TAY BRIDGE, he was relegated to runner-up on that punishing run to the line by DOUBLE CHANCE and JACK HORNER respectively. In 1927 he finished third on BRIGHT'S BOY, only two lengths behind SPRIG and BOVRIL III.

As a very successful trainer, he won the Cheltenham Gold Cup twice with the brilliant EASTER HERO and sent out BROWN TONY to win the 1930 Champion Hurdle. His elder brother, Ivor Anthony, trained both KELLSBORO' JACK in 1933 and ROYAL MAIL in 1937.

Tragically and ironically, John Randolph Anthony sustained a crippling injury stepping off a hack during a visit to America in the early 1950s. He died in 1954.

Above: ALLY SLOPER was the first National winner to be owned by a woman – Lady Nelson – and was superbly ridden to victory in 1915 by the leading amateur Jack Anthony

Brian Fletcher

If ever in the modern-day world of materialism a person's character was put totally and utterly to the extreme test, then a gentle, quietly-spoken man by the name of Brian Fletcher should be able to provide an enlightening dissertation on the subject.

But of course he wouldn't - he is far too modest and tolerant a person ever to dwell on the what-might-have-beens of life. Still more sadly, he is by far too absorbed in just getting by as what must surely be racing's forgotten man.

Born in 1948, still an austere time in north-eastern post-war Britain, Brian Fletcher came from working class stock and while still attending Barnard Castle Grammar School threw himself into the perilous activity of unauthorised flapping racing. Able to ride since his earliest years, Brian perfected his horsemanship in the hardest possible school, always dreaming that one day maybe he could rise to the dizzy heights of legitimate horse racing.

A chance meeting with Denys Smith, a recently licensed National Hunt trainer based at Bishop Auckland, was the answer to his prayers and in his first season with him in 1964/65 Brian rode three winners from twenty rides. Given a chance ride by Smith on the promising young RED ALLIGATOR, Brian rode the gelding to two convincing wins. So impressed with the young jockey were both owner and trainer, they agreed to Brian partnering the gelding in the forthcoming Grand National.

A rain-soaked Aintree that day in 1967 was the scene of the pile-up at the 23rd fence, when riderless POPHAM DOWN cut right across the leaders, bringing everything to a stand-still except the back-marker FOINAVON. With commendable determination, nineteen-year-old Fletcher persevered with RED ALLIGATOR to eventually get him over the obstacle and bravely run on to finish third behind FOINAVON and the favourite HONEY END. Without a loose horse to spoil the party the following year,

Fletcher gave RED ALLIGATOR a copybook ride to win the National by twenty lengths from MOIDORE'S TOKEN and Gregory Peck's DIFFERENT CLASS. Finishing that season with 77 winners, Brian Fletcher finished second in the jockeys' table behind champion Josh Gifford.

Although failing to get round in the next three Nationals, Fletcher remained in the top flight of northern-based jockeys throughout this period, until a terrible day in late February 1972 at Teeside Park racecourse. A crashing fall in a steeplechase left the young jockey unconscious with serious head injuries for ten days, and for many harrowing months his career seemed at an end. Only with an inbred determination and against doctor's advice, did Brian Fletcher finally begin the long haul back to steeplechasing. After a couple of confidence-boosting wins late in 1972, he was approached by Donald McCain who was looking for a regular partner for his rising star RED RUM.

To merely say the rest is history would be unfair to all concerned, for it is questionable if anyone other than Brian Fletcher could have beaten CRISP in the 1973 Grand National. With the runaway Australian champion leaving Becher's behind him second time round with a seeming unassailable lead, Fletcher alone realised the danger of leaving a pursuit any later. To overtake the leader in the final strides after looking well beaten was a tremendous achievement. To repeat the victory the next year with RED RUM, simply endorsed the rider's excellence at Aintree. After finishing second on 'Rummy' in 1975 and third with EYECATCHER in 1976, he hung up his boots on medical advice, yet remains an important member of the elite band of men to have graced Aintree with their deeds.

Right: A second victory for RED RUM in 1974 and a third for jockey Brian Fletcher who is being congratulated by fellow jockey Ron Barry

GREAT TRAINERS

Without owners, there wouldn't be horses. Without horses, trainers would not be required. Without either, jockeys would find themselves unwanted.

Above: Four times champion jockey, Fred Winter twice rode the winner of the race before winning it twice more as a trainer

Fortunately, there exist sufficient people who dream of achieving what few can aspire to - owning a horse considered good enough to carry their colours in the most famous steeplechase on earth.

John Elmore began it all when his LOTTERY carried everything before him, including success in that severest test of all. Since then, men of vision and the necessary funds to pursue their aims have found in the Grand National a means of registering their existence. Countless numbers have invested huge sums of money in the hope of leading in the winner of the most difficult equestrian event in the world. As the first to acquire such a distinction, John Elmore set the pattern for all to follow. For over 160 years multitudes of like-minded men and women have attempted to savour the sublime joy Elmore tasted with LOTTERY on that February day in 1839.

Such dignitaries as the Prince of Wales, Lord John Manners, Count Charles Kinsky, Frank Bibby and the Honourable Dorothy Paget all, in time, gained the knowledge of what victory in the great race could be and mean. That quest for National recognition remains to the present day.

A certain gentleman named Noel Le Mare inherited that dream and waited a lifetime to actually see it become reality, though when it did the rewards were threefold. For just £6,000, Le Mare experienced three times over the ecstasy most strive for without ever obtaining.

A foreigner in a strange land, Charles Kinsky was soon smitten with the allure of Aintree and its famous steeplechase and between exacting diplomatic duties, somehow found time to secure a dual victory by owning and riding ZOEDONE triumphantly in 1883.

The late purchase of brewer William Hall Walker in 1896 resulted in success not merely for the owner but also for the City of Liverpool, despite Mr Walker not even recognising his horse in the paddock. Unusually, a large portion of the fortunes of victory were allocated to a local art gallery.

With regard to the trainers, it is they who spend the sleepless nights tending to and preparing the horses in their care for the perils of the racecourse. They more than anyone else suffer a thousand deaths each time their runner falls, seems out of sorts or simply has an off day, and they alone hold a responsibility to the owner, jockey and most of all the animal. That most congenial of men, Fred Rimell, turned out a record four National winners, Tom Coulthwaite, Vincent O'Brien and Captain Tim Forster three each, and Jenny Pitman two heroes, in addition to another in 1993 which didn't count.

What the future hopefully holds is people with the same vision of a spring afternoon at Liverpool, when they stand atop the world and their days of dedication, uncertainty and hope are completely rewarded.

Below: GRAKLE is escorted back to the winner's enclosure by his trainer Tom Coulthwaite at the end of the 1931 Grand National. The gelding was the third and last National winner prepared by the Hednesford trainer

John Maunsell Richardson

Regrettably, details concerning trainers in the early years of the Grand National are either vague or non-existent, very probably for the same reason that some amateur riders chose to disguise their identities by using assumed names. It was all a matter of the unsavoury reputation associated with the sport during its development stage.

Below: The 1874 winner of the Grand National was REUGNY and this turned out to be the last ever public ride of John Maunsell Richardson

Even after the formation of the National Hunt Committee in 1866, certain trainers preferred their licences to be held under the names of their head lads, such as John Swatton, chief groom at the Bishop's Sutton stables where the great CLOISTER was prepared for his 1893 National victory. Although Swatton is credited as winning trainer in the record books, it was in fact his employer, the celebrated Arthur Yates, who trained the horse.

Former flat-race jockey George Dockeray, who rode LAP-DOG to victory in the 1826 Epsom Derby, trained both LOTTERY in 1839 and MISS MOWBRAY thirteen years later to gain

success in the famous Liverpool steeplechase. But by far the most prominent and colourful English trainer of the nineteenth century was Lincolnshire-born John Maunsell Richardson.

Educated at Harrow and Cambridge, Richardson was a natural athlete who proved himself a most capable runner, jumper and cricketer while still quite young. At both fencing and racquets he was almost unbeatable. It was while at Cambridge, however, that his attention turned to horses and in no time at all 'Cat' Richardson, as he was known to his friends, became one of the finest and most polished amateur riders of his era. While still an undergraduate and barely nineteen years old, he rode his first steeplechase winner at Huntingdon. Without neglecting his studies, he quickly built such a reputation for himself among the chasing fraternity that his services became greatly sought after by owners and trainers.

Setting up as a trainer near his birthplace at Limber Magna, Richardson in 1871 befriended the Yorkshireman Captain James Machell, whose interests involved trading and training horses, managing them and most seriously of all, backing them. Often the scourge of the bookmakers, Machell was a very shrewd gambler, preferring to keep his intended investments completely to himself until the very last moment before a race to secure the longest odds possible. Captain Machell could also be a fiery and very abrasive character.

Having given the Captain's six-year-old DISTURBANCE a thorough preparation, John Maunsell Richardson not only saddled the horse for the 1873 Grand National but then weighed-out to ride it in the race. Much to the delight of Machell, his representative was almost ignored in the betting and it was largely due to his late bets that DISTURBANCE went off at 20/1. Bringing his mount with a well-timed challenge at the final obstacle, 'The Cat' took DISTURBANCE past the post six lengths clear of his nearest rival. What should have been a double celebration victory the following year, unfortunately degenerated into an acrimonious and most undignified slanging match even before the race began. Having trained Captain Machell's REUGNY to perfection for Aintree, Richardson apparently made little secret of his

confidence in the horse to his friends and neighbours and by the time the owner made his way to the bookies, REUGNY had been made 5/1 favourite. Furious in the extreme, Captain Machell accused his trainer/rider of skull-duggery, adding the final insult by stating: 'I don't keep horses for damned Lincolnshire farmers to bet on'.

Offering to give up the ride on REUGNY, Richardson changed his mind, won the race by six lengths, but was so hurt by the unfair accusations he never rode again.

Above: Born in Lincolnshire, John Maunsell Richardson was a natural athlete who began riding in hunter races while studying at Cambridge, and soon became recognised as an amateur of the highest calibre

Tom Coulthwaite

Like the horses they care for, trainers come in all shapes, sizes and, very definitely, temperaments. Look no further than the man destined to become known as 'The Grand Old Man of British Chasing'.

Tom Coulthwaite was born in Lancashire in 1862, never sat on a horse in his life and before becoming involved with them, was a highly successful trainer of athletes of the human variety. An extremely blunt, eccentric character, he was though a rather reserved and quietly generous man respected by all who knew him, especially his stable staff.

Right: Tom Coulthwaite first entered sport as a trainer of human athletes and by employing the same principles with horses, was soon turning out winners over fences on a regular basis. He was 45 years old when saddling his first Aintree winner in 1907, the late-developer EREMON and repeated the process three years later when winning the race again for the same owner – Mr Stanley Howard – with JENKINSTOWN

Upon turning his training talents to racehorses, Coulthwaite set up a yard at Hednesford in Staffordshire in the early years of the twentieth century. In 1907 he saddled a virtual novice named EREMON in the National. Despite having only been racing for twelve months, the gelding was a strongly fancied 8/1 chance but from the very first fence his jockey Alfred Newey became involved in a nightmare ride. Having broken a stirrup leather at the initial obstacle, Newey found himself in the lead from an early point, though after jumping the Canal Turn the riderless horse RATHVALE drew alongside and for the remainder of the journey attempted to bite and savage EREMON. For a whole circuit the intruder posed a constant threat, despite Newey trying desperately to fend him off with his whip. It was only at the second Valentine's that EREMON finally raced clear, going on to win by six lengths from TOM WEST and PATLANDER.

Coulthwaite sent out his second big Aintree winner in 1910 when a snow-squall swept the racecourse as the runners paraded, with the brilliant 6/1 favourite and top weight JERRY M leading them. In an exciting dual through the final mile between JERRY M and Coulthwaite's JENKINSTOWN, the latter, in receipt of 30 pounds from the favourite, prevailed to win by three lengths. Standing in the winner's enclosure that National day the trainer had every reason to feel proud for just 24 hours earlier he had welcomed there his RATHNALLY after its triumph in the Stanley Chase over one circuit of the National course.

The roof fell in on Tom Coulthwaite's world in 1913 when an investigation by the National Hunt Committee into the running of two of his horses, led to his being warned off.

Deprived of his chosen livelihood until after the Great War, Coulthwaite regained his licence to

carry on where he left off, turning out winners on a very regular basis. By now a much respected figure on the steeplechasing scene, a regular visitor to his yard was the Prince of Wales who rode out with his string and afterwards, high on his Cannock Chase gallops, Coulthwaite would entertain His Royal Highness with the 'customary dram' in the retreat he called his 'Castle' – a corrugated iron hut.

Nothing could have been more appropriate for Coulthwaite than his third National winner to be one of his favourite horses, GRAKLE, who in 1931 won the race by one and a half lengths from a former inhabitant of Coulthwaite's Hednesford yard, GREGALACH. Retiring in 1932, Tom Coulthwaite died in 1948 a credit to his profession, as was confirmed by Haydock Park's executive naming a steeplechase after him.

Above: Yorkshireman Bob Chadwick proudly sits astride the 1910 National winner JENKINSTOWN, Coulthwaite's second training success in the race

Fred Rimmell

If ever a man was born to the saddle and the world of steeplechasing, then that man was Fred Rimell. Born in 1913, the son of Kinnersley trainer Tom Rimell, he became apprenticed to his father and rode 34 flat-race winners before turning his attention to jump racing when nineteen years old. It may be mere coincidence, but that year of 1932 saw his father saddling the winner of the National, FORBRA.

Below: Fred Rimell's E.S.B. lies third over the Water Jump in the 1956 National on the fateful day when DEVON LOCH inexplicably collapsed just yards from the post with the race at his mercy. DEVON LOCH is seen right behind E.S.B. at the halfway stage

Rimell junior made a very positive impact himself as a jump jockey, winning the jockeys' championship on no less than four occasions until, in 1947, he broke his neck twice in the space of eight months, bringing a premature conclusion to his riding career.

Recovering slowly, Rimell eventually took over his father's licence at Kinnersley and in no time at all was among the leading trainers in the land. In 1956 his E.S.B. benefited from the Queen Mother's runner DEVON LOCH's collapse just 50 yards from the finish of the National, thus providing Fred with his first winner in the race.

Five years later in 1961, his success with the grey NICOLAUS SILVER was gained completely on individual merit, giving jockey Bobby Beasley success in the race exactly 70 years after his grandfather Harry's victory on COME AWAY.

In 1970 GAY TRIP, who had never won beyond two and a half miles, gave a perfect display over Aintree's huge fences, providing his jockey Pat Taaffe with a second victory in the race and trainer Rimell with his third.

With a yard literally overflowing with equine stars, Fred Rimell captured every major prize in National Hunt racing during his lengthy career as a trainer. Every jockey going out on a horse prepared by the 'Master of Kinnersley' could rest assured his mount was well schooled and as fit as could be.

In the summer of 1975 the Kinnersley yard welcomed a newcomer, the nine-year-old gelding RAG TRADE, who after finishing tenth behind L'ESCARGOT in the most recent National was transferred by owner Mr Paul Raymond to the care of Fred Rimell. Allowing the gelding time to return to some kind of decent form, the trainer was rewarded for his patience at Chepstow, with RAG TRADE somewhat luckily winning the Welsh Grand

National. Concentrating on having the horse spot-on for Aintree, Rimell avoided any other races and just a few weeks before the Liverpool fixture received a boost to his plans when saddling ROYAL FROLIC to win the Cheltenham Gold Cup.

Partnered in the National by Irishman John Burke, RAG TRADE attracted enough support in the betting to start 14/1 in the 32-runner field. Kept in mid-division for most of the way, he began making progress on the run back to the final two fences. With RED RUM holding a slight advantage over EYECATCHER, CEOL-NA-MARA and THE DIKLER jumping the last fence, the cheers rang out as it appeared RED RUM was about to score an unbelievable third success. Running on courageously in the final 200 yards, though, RAG TRADE got up to beat RED RUM by two lengths, with EYECATCHER staying on to be third.

It was a fitting climax to a most thrilling race and an incredible twenty years in which Fred Rimell sent out four Grand National winners. That is a record likely to last for many years to come.

Above: Fred's father, Thomas Reginald Rimell, was a highly successful trainer under both codes of racing and in 1932 saddled the 50/1 shot FORBRA to win the National

Neville Crump

While serving with the 4th Hussars from 1931 until 1935, Neville Crump rode regularly as an amateur and before taking out a trainer's licence himself in 1937, was employed as assistant to JL Hall at his Russley Park stables. Sadly, though, like countless others at that point in Britain's history, his career had to be put on hold as a result of the Second World War. Through the entire period of hostilities, Neville Crump served with distinction in the Royal Armoured Corps and despite the lengthy interruption to his trade, soon established himself in the world of National Hunt racing.

Within three years of returning to his Middleham headquarters, Captain Crump saddled the latest addition to his string for the 1948 Grand National, the nine-year-old bay mare SHEILA'S COTTAGE. Partnered by the superb Irish jockey Arthur Thompson, she was almost ignored in the betting at 50/1, largely because of her gender, for no mare had won the race since SHANNON LASS in 1902. The only other mare opposing Crump's charge at Aintree was at even longer odds, ZAHIA being returned at 100/1 and coming to the penultimate fence it was she who looked certain to win. An error on the part of her jockey, however, who in taking the wrong course ran out before the final obstacle, left SHEILA'S COTTAGE the easiest of tasks in out-running FIRST OF THE DANDIES to the post. Always considered by trainer Crump as an 'ornery old cow', she nonetheless provided him with his first National victory, even though two days after her success the horse rewarded her jockey by biting off his thumb.

Now established as a man who knew his profession well, Neville Crump went from strength to strength, winning the Scottish

Below: The always popular FREEBOOTER slips up on landing at the second Canal Turn in 1952, leaving TEAL to provide trainer Neville Crump with a second success in the race

Left: Captain Crump's first National winner in 1948 was SHEILA'S COTTAGE at 50/1, ridden by that fine Aintree specialist Arthur Thompson

Grand National with WOT NO SUN in 1949 and the Welsh equivalent two years later with SKYREHOLME.

In 1952 a large field of 47 runners charged the starting tape in the National, causing a delay of some twelve minutes before the race could begin. By the time it was repaired, jockey Arthur Thompson aboard Captain Crump's TEAL shouted to on-lookers that: 'I thought I would have been in the winner's enclosure by now'. Although later than anticipated, sure enough Thompson returned triumphantly with TEAL to a hero's welcome after a perfect display of jumping in dreadful conditions. To round off the celebrations, Neville Crump's other contestant - WOT NO SUN - finished in third place.

After learning the art of jumping in the hunting field, the bay gelding MERRYMAN II was sent to Middelham as an eight-year-old to be prepared as a steeplechaser. After winning both the Liverpool Foxhunters' Chase and the Scottish Grand National in 1959, he arrived at Aintree the following March the 13/2 favourite for the big race itself. Although nobody knew it, it was to be the last National over the old-style upright obstacles. Jumping like a stag throughout, MERRYMAN II won a very exciting race by fifteen lengths ridden by Crump's former apprentice jockey Gerry Scott.

After a long and successful career which saw him turn out the winners of almost every long-distance chase in the land, including three Grand Nationals, Captain Neville Crump finally retired and sadly passed away in 1997.

Left: MERRYMAN II makes his way to the unsaddling ring after scoring a fifteen-length triumph in the 1960 race. The gelding is accompanied by winning owner Miss Winifred Wallace, trainer Neville Crump and, of course, the man who so expertly guided him round, jockey Gerry Scott

Fred Winter

One of only a handful of men to have been champion jockey and subsequently leading trainer, Fred Winter also holds the distinction of being the first trainer to win over £100,000 for his owners in a single season.

The son of a famous flat-race jockey, Fred himself began his own career riding winners on the flat before increasing weight made him turn his attention to competing over fences. In 1947 he won first time out over obstacles on his father's horse CARTON. After a long recovery from a serious injury, the budding jockey teamed up with Findon trainer Ryan Price and from there on the partnership for many years was virtually invincible. Together they were successful in almost every major National Hunt event and in 1957 Fred rode his first Grand National winner on SUNDEW, although the man who saddled that winner was Henley-in-Arden trainer Frank Hudson.

After finishing a good fifth on the Ryan Price-trained KILMORE in the 1961 National, a repeat effort was made twelve months later on heavy Aintree going and amid persistent snow flurries. In one of the most gruelling contests seen for many years, four horses came to the final fence almost in line, but on touching down safely Winter romped away with KILMORE to win comfortably by ten lengths from WYNDBURGH, MR WHAT and GAY NAVARREE. It was one of the jockey's proudest moments in racing, for he had made no secret of his wish to win the National for his guv'nor Ryan Price.

Less than three months later came what many experts consider Fred Winter's greatest

Below: Eight lengths clear of Scottish-trained WYNDBURGH, SUNDEW passes the winning post the 20/1 winner. Fred Winter again rode the winner in 1962 on KILMORE, once more relegating WYNDBURGH to second place

exhibition of horsemanship when riding MANDARIN to victory in the Grande Steeplechase de Paris. For more than three miles the jockey guided the small gelding over the difficult twisting course with a broken bridle, yet not only succeeded in getting round but, despite himself suffering a stomach disorder, produced MANDARIN brilliantly to succeed in a photo finish.

After retiring from the saddle in 1964, he was awarded the CBE for his services to racing and after his application for a position as an assistant starter was turned down, took out a trainer's licence and began his operations from Uplands in Lambourn.

If Winter's success as a jockey had been swift, his rise as a racehorse trainer of immense distinction was simply meteoric. One of the first residents of his new yard was the American gelding JAY TRUMP, a dual winner of the prestigious Maryland Hunt Cup. In addition to preparing him for a tilt at the National, Winter was also charged with teaching his part owner and rider Tommy Smith how to adapt to the different forms of obstacles in this country. Both horse and rider did the former champion jockey proud, galloping on well in the closing stages to beat the hot favourite FREDDIE by three quarters of a length.

Just twelve months later in 1965, Fred Winter led in his second Grand National winner in only his second season as a trainer, when the flat-race reject ANGLO ran out the

clearest of winners by twenty lengths from the favourite again, FREDDIE.

He became leading trainer for the first time in the 1970/71 season, an achievement he was to repeat on numerous occasions before suffering a stroke at home in August 1987 which brought the incredible racing career of Fred Winter to an end. In the 40 years since scoring his first jumping success, Winter had captured the hearts of a grateful racing public as a jockey, trainer and one of the finest ambassadors ever to grace a racecourse with his presence.

Left: On a rain-soaked day in 1957 jockey Fred Winter crowned his career by adding the Grand National to his tally of big race wins

Below: In his first season as a trainer, Winter prepared the American challenger JAY TRUMP to win a thrilling National in 1965

Tim Forster

Tim Forster was born in 1934 and after serving as an officer with the 11th Hussars between 1954 and 1960, went as a pupil to leading Newmarket trainer Geoffrey Brooke before moving on to become assistant to Derek Candy. Striking out on his own with a trainer's licence in 1962, Captain Forster began with a smallish stable of jumpers at Letcombe Regis on the edge of the Berkshire Downs.

Below: Irish challenger GREASEPAINT leads LAST SUSPECT over the last fence in 1985. At this stage the strongly fancied MR SNUGFIT was several lengths clear but ridden out by jockey Hywel Davies, LAST SUSPECT relentlessly battled on to score a shock 50/1 victory by a length and a half

Quickly establishing himself, his first really good horse was a tough hunter-chaser called BAULKING GREEN who proved a model of consistency by winning 22 chases. Others from his yard to distinguish themselves over the sticks included ROYAL MARSHALL, RUEIL, DENYS ADVENTURE and the 1965 Fred Withington Chase winner MR WONDERFUL.

Upon the death of one of his owners, Mrs Heather Sumner, Tim Forster discovered that as a beneficiary of her will he had inherited the chestnut gelding he had purchased on her behalf five years earlier, WELL TO DO. Holding a qualification for the 1972 Grand National, the horse duly took his place in the line-up for the race and ten months after the death of Mrs

Sumner, WELL TO DO out-stayed previous winner of the race GAY TRIP for a two-length victory.

American-owned BEN NEVIS did most of his racing in the United States, where he remained unbeaten in twelve races including the Maryland Hunt Cup. After his second success in that event, he was sent back to England to be trained by Tim Forster for Liverpool's famous steeplechase. Strongly fancied for the 1979 race, BEN NEVIS was caught up in the mêlée at the Chair which caused the elimination of nine contestants. Now all hopes for National glory were pinned on the 1980 event.

By now twelve years old, without a single victory from twelve attempts since returning to Europe, and with the state of the ground being considered against him, BEN NEVIS at 40/1 was thought to have no chance at all in the first National of the eighties. Ridden by merchant banker Charlie Fenwick, son-in-law of the gelding's owner, BEN NEVIS was gently coasted round on the first circuit before making a forward move early on the second circuit. The heavy going having reduced the field to just a handful of runners, BEN NEVIS took control jumping Becher's for the second time. Seemingly completely at ease with his task, he romped home twenty lengths clear of just three other survivors.

During the heady days of the mighty ARKLE during the 1960s, his owner Anne, Duchess of Westminster, had vehemently refused to allow the horse to take part in any Grand National because of the dangers involved. Twenty years later, however, with the race decidedly less treacherous, she felt less unease about entering her eleven-year-old LAST SUSPECT for the 1985 race. There could never be, of course, any comparison between the two horses, for the triple Gold Cup winner was in a brilliant class of his own, whereas on his most recent form LAST SUSPECT had frequently displayed an annoying distaste for racing.

After pulling himself up on his last outing, both the owner and Tim Forster decided to withdraw the gelding from the National and it was only jockey Hywel Davies who eventually persuaded the owner to allow him to take his chance at Aintree. Giving a foot-perfect display of jumping, LAST SUSPECT produced a storming

Left: Taking out his first licence in 1962, Tim Forster saddled WELL TO DO to provide his first National winner in 1972. BEN NEVIS in 1980 and LAST SUSPECT in 1985 brought his total of National victories to a very respectable three

late run after the last fence to catch and beat the clear leader MR SNUGFIT in the very last strides.

It was trainer Tim Forster's third and final Grand National winner and a most fitting tribute to a man who contributed so much to National Hunt racing. After a lengthy illness he sadly died in April 1999.

Below: WELL TO DO, on the right, issues his challenge at the final fence in 1972, going on to win by two lengths from the former winner GAY TRIP

The IRISH are COMING

11

**GRAND®
NATIONAL**

— AINTREE —

WITH HINDSIGHT, it appears obvious after such famous prominent Irish racing men as Tom Ferguson, the Marquis of Waterford and Alan McDonough revealed such interest in the early Nationals, that for once every year Aintree would become the centre of attention for all from the Emerald Isle.

Spurred on by the deeds of their first Grand National winner MATTHEW, and in spite of early reservations concerning the severity of the race, the Irish – whose close affinity with the horse is legendary – seem to have made a devout commitment to crossing the Irish Sea each spring and gaining National fame.

Left: PAPILLON leads MELY MOSS towards the end of the 2000 National

There can be little doubt that the contribution made by Irishmen and the great horses they so brilliantly breed have added immeasurably to the allure of the Grand National. Statistics will show that even if English owned, trained and ridden, the majority of winners of Liverpool's formidable steeplechase are horses which have drawn their first breath in Ireland.

Names such as ABD-EL-KADER, CORTOLVIN, THE LAMB, TROYTOWN, EARLY MIST, ROYAL TAN and QUARE TIMES roll off the tongue like those of much loved sons, daughters and grand-children to those who appreciate just what is the true mark of equestrian greatness – victory in the roughest, toughest, most demanding race of all. A far larger volume than this would still find it hard to fully define the considerable importance of Irish involvement in the development, traditions and romance of the Grand National, so instead of an all-out gallop we will limit ourselves to more of a steady canter.

Henry Eyre Linde was one of the earliest of what came to be known as 'public trainers' and despite some criticism regarding his rather harsh methods, certainly became the greatest of his profession in Ireland. The comparatively new practice of using public trainers came about mainly as a result of the Land Acts, which brought about the decline of huge estates owned by aristocratic gentlemen. Whereas formerly they had their horses prepared for racing by grooms in their employ, with the depletion of their land it became less expensive to use the services of professional trainers and it was soon discovered to be more profitable also. They suddenly began winning more races with horses saddled by the likes of Henry Eyre Linde, Garrett Moore and the very promising Beasley family, due mainly to the use of more sophisticated methods.

Another development resulting from the growing army of public trainers which benefited the sport, came with an increase of racehorse ownership from the like of bankers, merchants and businessmen in general.

With Linde and Garrett Moore using specially-built steeplechase courses on their gallops to acquaint horses with the hazards they would encounter, their approach to getting an animal ready for a contest was both revolutionary and enormously successful. Another tremendous advantage these men held over their rivals was having the services of such excellent horsemen as Garrett Moore himself, together with his brother Willie, and in Linde's case the formidable Beasley brothers.

It was in 1879 that THE LIBERATOR first drew English attention to the fact that a new and formidable force of challengers was about to descend on Aintree from across the Irish Sea. A difficult horse to both train and ride, THE LIBERATOR was described by John Maunsell Richardson as 'a cunning old devil', yet Garrett Moore brought the horse to Liverpool so fit and in such good form that the gelding started 5/1 second favourite. There was a last-minute hiccup when a former part-owner of the horse, a Mr Plunkett Taaffe, sought an injunction to prevent THE LIBERATOR taking part. The application was refused by the Master of the Rolls and Garrett Moore gave his mount a perfect ride over the big fences to win by ten lengths. Shortly after his Grand National triumph Garrett Moore gave up riding to concentrate on training. Moving to England, he set up a successful yard specialising in preparing flat-race horses. The family's link with Aintree, however, was maintained by his younger brother Willie.

Henry Eyre Linde can be claimed justly as the one man above all others who made the 1880s the 'Golden Age' of Irish steeplechasing. After a period of service with the Royal Irish Constabulary, Linde took up residence at Eryefield Lodge, the Curragh, and quickly proved himself an exceptional handler of thoroughbreds. So famous did his establishment become, that Empress Elizabeth of Austria included it on her hunting tour of Ireland in 1879. Fittingly, it was a chestnut mare named after her who provided both trainer Linde and amateur rider Tommy Beasley with their first taste of Grand National glory in 1880. Judiciously ridden, the mare EMPRESS was kept towards the rear of the field for much of the contest, only moving into contention on the approach to the final two obstacles. Producing the better turn of foot, EMPRESS swept past the long-time leader JUPITER TONANS, landed in front over the last and raced on for a two-length victory over the previous year's winner THE LIBERATOR. Twelve months on, it was almost a carbon copy victory again for the trainer and his brilliant rider, this time scored with seven-year-old 11/2 joint-favourite WOODBROOK, and in 1882 they came agonisingly close to making it a hat-trick of wins in three successive years. Represented on that occasion by CYRUS, they were beaten by just a head in the final yards by SEAMAN, ridden by his owner

Lord John Manners of the Grenadier Guards. The most ironic aspect of the defeat was that SEAMAN had been sold to Lord Manners just four months before the National by none other than Henry Eyre Linde. In addition to saddling winners of the race, Linde also sent out the runner-up five times and so great was his reputation, other trainers often requested the use of his training facilities, particularly when preparing a horse for Aintree. The replica course he had built at the Curragh, with copies of Becher's, Valentine's and The Chair, was the envy of many, and one horse often schooled over it was the mare FRIGATE. Having finished third in the National three times, she appeared destined to be always the bridesmaid but never the bride. That is until her owner-breeder Matthew Maher of Ballinkeele, County Wexford, received permission to train her over

Linde's miniature 'Aintree'. With Tommy Beasley in the saddle, in 1889 FRIGATE at last achieved the victory she had so richly earned, bravely holding on in a desperate finish to win by a length from WHY NOT.

Sadly afflicted with Bright's disease, Henry Eyre Linde died on 18 March 1897, leaving a legacy of brilliance for future generations of trainers to echo and memories of his magical Aintree years.

Carrying on where his elder brother Garrett left off, Willie Moore brought the family name back into prominence in the final decade of the nineteenth century, first with a gelding who many considered had long left his best days behind him. Although by then with his training headquarters at Weyhill in Hampshire, Willie remained Irish through and through. Allowing his licence to train to be

Above: Harry Beasley both trained and rode the pride of the Irish COME AWAY to win the 1891 National, conceding five pounds to the runner-up, the brilliant CLOISTER

Far left: At seventeen-and-a-half hands high THE LIBERATOR towered over his seventeen rivals in the 1879 National, in stature and performance, winning by a comfortable ten lengths

held in the name of his head-lad, John Collins, was typical of the man. Of the fourteen runners in the 1894 Grand National WHY NOT was, at thirteen years of age, far and away the most experienced and despite his missed chances in four previous attempts, Willie Moore had brought him to a peak of fitness at precisely the right time. Having won his last four races, including Aintree's Grand Sefton Chase, WHY NOT went off joint-favourite at 5/1 with NELLY GRAY. Splendidly ridden by Arthur Nightingall, WHY NOT moved to the front after jumping Becher's for the second

time, just behind the leader LADY ELLEN II. Hugging the inner rail all the way back, he took up the running at the penultimate fence, only to be at once challenged by the pride of Waterford, WILD MAN FROM BORNEO. Fighting back with great determination, WHY NOT regained his advantage to pass the post a length and a half in front of LADY ELLEN II, with WILD MAN FROM BORNEO a head back in third place. The winner was conceding over two stone in weight to the runner-up. Evergreen WHY NOT took his Grand National tally to seven by competing again in the race in both 1895 and 1896, finishing in fifth place on each occasion.

Again in the National winner's enclosure in 1896, Willie Moore this time received a tremendous local ovation, for his winner was the Liverpool-owned THE SOARER. Rounding off the nineteenth century in the same jubilant manner, Moore produced the mighty MANIFESTO to the height of his brilliance to win the 1899 Grand National under the massive burden of twelve stone seven pounds. Upon his retirement, Willie Moore was succeeded by his nephew Frank Hartigan, who had formerly assisted him at Weyhill. In 1930 Hartigan followed his uncle's fine example by training the Liverpool-owned SHAUN GOILIN to win a very hard-fought National.

After setting up as a public trainer at Ringwood, Jack Ruttle persuaded leading show-jump rider Tim Hyde to transfer his talents to the racecourse in order to partner the gelding WORKMAN in the 1939 Grand National. Having once changed hands for the meagre sum of 25 guineas, WORKMAN had developed into a fine staying chaser, finishing third in the 1938 race behind BATTLESHIP, and with Tim Hyde they duly won the 1939 National in impressive style. Jockey Hyde so relished the heady atmosphere of steeplechasing that he remained a part of it until 1951 when a fall in a race ended his career. Apart from his victory with WORKMAN, he is best remembered for the partnership he struck up with PRINCE REGENT, on whom he won the 1946 Cheltenham Gold Cup and finished third and fourth in both the 1946 and 1947 Nationals. It was the latter of these events which saw the unknown 100/1 outsider CAUGHOO amaze the thousands of Aintree

spectators by romping home to win the race by twenty lengths.

The phenomenal success of Michael Vincent O'Brien since he first took out a trainer's licence in 1944 has become a fascinating and important element of recent racing history, under both codes of the sport. Initially concentrating his ability on National Hunt racing, the 'Master of Ballydoyle', as O'Brien was soon to become known, carried off every major jumping prize on offer in the space of ten short years. Renowned for his regular raids on the Cheltenham Festival, O'Brien trained the winner of the Cheltenham Gold Cup four times, that of the Champion Hurdle on three occasions and, in addition, sent out horses to succeed in no less than ten divisions of the Gloucestershire Hurdle. It was in 1951 that he first came close to adding the Grand National to his score of big race conquests, when sending out the seven-year-old chestnut ROYAL TAN to compete in what became known as 'The All Fall Down National'. From a disastrous start, with at

least a third of the 36 runners facing the wrong way when the barrier went up, only two horses with jockeys returned to the racecourse for the final time. ROYAL TAN, with his trainer's brother 'Phonsie' in the saddle, appeared to have the race well in his grasp until an error at the last fence allowed his sole rival, the mare NICKEL COIN, to race clear to a six-length victory. Again the following year it was the last obstacle which proved his undoing, ROYAL TAN falling there when certain of finishing third. Vincent O'Brien's better fancied EARLY MIST fell at the first fence that year, but in 1953 when ridden by that superb Irish-born jockey Bryan Marshall, the combination proved unbeatable, with EARLY MIST achieving a twenty-length victory from the former Gold Cup winner MONT TREMBLANT. In winning the 1954 National at his third attempt, ROYAL TAN had to dig deep for reserves of stamina in that desperately close finish with Yorkshire-trained TUDOR LINE, yet with Bryan Marshall again proving his mastery in the saddle, the 'Master of Ballydoyle' led in his second

Below: The excellence of horsemanship as practised by two of its finest exponents. Richard Dunwoody on CALL IT A DAY holds a fractional advantage over Paul Carberry aboard BOBBYJO, but it is the latter who sprints clear for the first Irish-trained victory in 24 years

successive National winner. Having already broken virtually every record in National Hunt racing, Vincent O'Brien made a four-pronged attack to create another at Aintree on 26 March 1955. In addition to his two proven Aintree horses, EARLY MIST and ROYAL TAN, his Liverpool newcomers ORIENTAL WAY and QUARE TIMES also made up the 30-runner field on ground so rain-sodden it resembled a quagmire. Given the most perfect of rides by the rising star of Irish jumping Pat Taaffe, QUARE TIMES overcame the gruelling conditions to win by twelve lengths from TUDOR LINE and CAREY'S COTTAGE, the latter having been trained by winning jockey Pat Taaffe's father Thomas and ridden by his brother 'Tos'.

Of many great moments in the career of Vincent O'Brien, that hat-trick of successive Grand National victories placed him at the peak of professional perfection and his complete switch to flat racing in 1959 left

jump racing the poorer. He remains, however, the only man to have saddled three different horses to win the world's greatest steeplechase three times on the trot.

Considered by many pundits little more than a novice when facing the starter in the 1958 race, eight-year-old MR WHAT caused more than a few red faces when romping home the winner by 30 lengths, although the late rush of money placed on him was an indication of Irish confidence in the trainer Thomas J Taaffe, Pat's father. It was to be another seventeen years before an Irish-trained horse won the National again and the only consolation for those across the Irish Sea in that time was the success in the race of such jockeys as Bobby Beasley, Willie Robinson, Eddie Harty and the immaculate Pat Taaffe, who scored his second Grand National victory at the age 40 on GAY TRIP in 1970.

In relegating RED RUM into second place in the 1975 Grand National, the dual Cheltenham Gold Cup winner L'ESCARGOT not only denied 'Rummy' a third victory in the race but became the first Irish-trained winner since MR WHAT in 1958. He was also the last for 24 years.

With typical Aintree coincidence, BOBBYJO was ridden to victory with absolute aplomb by that complete stylist Paul Carberry in the 1999 National, his father Tommy having trained the horse. It was Tommy, of course, who guided L'ESCARGOT home in 1975 and to further emphasise young Mr Carberry's pedigree, his grandfather Dan Moore came very close to winning the 1938 race on ROYAL DANIELI, beaten by only a head by BATTLESHIP. Twelve months later, the first National of the 21st century repeated the process for the Emerald Isle, when Ruby Walsh rode the product of his father Ted's preparation PAPILLON to success.

Above: Never known to do things by half, the Irish capture their second successive National with jockey Ruby Welsh reacting in a suitable manner as PAPILLON carries him to victory in 2000. Fellow Irishman Norman Williamson is a worthy second on MELY MOSS

OVERSEAS
CONNECTIONS

FROM ITS EARLIEST YEARS
the Grand National had attracted the attention of foreign owners. In 1856 Frenchman Baron de la Motte was represented in the race by two horses, FRANC PICARD and JEAN DU QUESNE, the latter actually going off the 9/2 favourite. Although neither managed to finish the course, Aintree's big steeplechase had undoubtedly caught the imagination of racing men across the English Channel.

Left: The smallest horse with the tallest and youngest jockey, American-bred and owned BATTLESHIP proved his heart was bigger than his body when courageously battling on to win the 1938 race by a head. Jockey Bruce Hobbs was the son of his mount's trainer Reg Hobbs

It was HUNTSMAN's victory in 1862 which provided the first French owner with a National triumph, the gentleman in question being the nobleman Viscount de Namur, who employed Yorkshire-born Harry Lamplugh to both train and ride his horses.

Having ridden many winners in France since going to live there as a teenager, Lamplugh is reputed to have assisted in the training of MISS MOWBRAY before her Liverpool success in 1852. Whatever the truth of this claim may be, the records do show that he was a fine jockey and a very capable trainer.

Though quite a number of winners of the great steeplechase have had humble careers on the flat, it is highly unlikely that any could equal the ignominy suffered by the French-bred horse ALCIBIADE in the early years of his racing life. So little ability did the chestnut display, he finished up running in a humble selling plate at Epsom out of which he was bought and subsequently became the property of Benjamin John ('Cherry') Angell. In a tremendous neck-and-neck finish with HALL COURT, ALCIBIADE won the 1865 Grand National by a head to become not just the first French-bred horse to succeed in the race, but also the first five-year-old to do so. Another National winner bred across the English Channel was REUGNY, owned by Captain Machell and ridden by John Maunsell Richardson. It was the fact that REUGNY started as favourite which led to the acrimonious break-up of the owner and rider partnership.

The finest example of how the allure of the Grand National can influence and govern a man's future is the story of the second son of one of the oldest and most noble families in Europe. Count Charles Kinsky was born in 1859 in Bohemia, Hungary, the son of a princess of Liechtenstein whose fame as a brilliant horsewoman was widespread and who was determined that her children should have the finest riding instructor available. Her choice fell to an English Master of Horse named Rowland Reynolds and it was this former cavalry officer who

educated the four sons and four daughters of the Princess to the highest level of equestrianism. His most attentive and responsive pupil by far was Charles, who not only acquired the delicate art of correctly balancing a horse but more significantly, Rowland Reynolds completely besotted his young protégé with inspirational tales of Liverpool's great steeplechase.

His opportunity to visit England came in 1878 when his diplomatic duties required him to accompany Empress Elizabeth of Austria on her hunting tour. It was during that trip that Charles Kinsky first saw the horse who was to turn his fondest dream into unimaginable reality. Witnessing the mare ZOEDONE win a small Hunt Steeplechase at the Ash Hunt in Cheshire, the young Count was so impressed with her that after winning a sizeable sum on the success of CORRIE ROY in the 1882 Cesarewitch, he bought her. By this time based at the Austro-Hungarian Embassy in London, Count Kinsky spent all his spare time schooling ZOEDONE on the gallops of his trainer W Jenkins at Upton. Two months after winning the Great Sandown Steeplechase on her by twenty lengths, Kinsky guided ZOEDONE to a ten-length victory in the 1883 Grand National. Finishing fifth in the race the following year, ZOEDONE was strongly fancied to repeat her National success in 1885 but to prevent her doing so she was most despicably poisoned on the way to the start. With the outbreak of the Great War in 1914, Prince Kinsky – as he was by then – had to return to his homeland to serve against the British Army. However, rather than enter into conflict with people he had come to like and admire, he volunteered for service on the Russian Front and when hostilities ceased, found himself in a Europe completely changed from the one he loved. The estates his family had governed for centuries were now part of a newly-formed country called Czechoslovakia. He died a sad and forlorn man in 1919, still grateful for his friendship with the English Master of Horse, Rowland Reynolds, and nostalgically proud of a ride on ZOEDONE one spring day at Liverpool.

In 1904 the wealthy New Zealand businessman Spencer Gollan sent his promising young chaser MOIFAA on a lengthy sea voyage, with Liverpool and the National his final destination. Shipwrecked en route, MOIFAA was considered lost at sea for some little time, until found stranded on an outcrop of land some distance from the southern coast of Ireland. Rescued and quickly restored to fitness, MOIFAA went on to win the 1904 Grand National by eight lengths.

Californian-bred RUBIO arrived in England as a yearling destined for the Newmarket Sales and after being sold there for just 15 guineas, eventually became the property of Major Frank Douglas-Pennant. After winning three chases as a five-year-old, the gelding broke down and despite advice from friends that RUBIO was beyond any further use as a jumper, Major Douglas-Pennant sent him to a friend who owned a hotel in Towcester, accompanied by some strange instructions. They were that the gelding should be used to pull the hotel bus to the railway station and back each day. This unusual form of road work restored the horse to fitness and put back into training with Fred Withington at Danebury in Hampshire, RUBIO joined his better fancied stable companion MATTIE MACGREGOR in a tilt at the 1908 National. A rank outsider at 66/1, RUBIO romped home to win comfortably by ten lengths from MATTIE MACGREGOR, the first American-bred horse to succeed in the race.

Another French-bred horse became the toast of the country of his birth in 1909, for LUTTEUR III was also owned and ridden by fellow countrymen. Owned by James Hennessy and with Georges Parfrement aboard, the five-year-old gelding started joint second favourite with SHADY GIRL at 100/9 and after giving a faultless display of jumping, passed the post two lengths in front of runner-up JUDAS.

During the Roaring Twenties, American racehorse owners stretched their interests to Liverpool and its famous steeplechase, often investing vast sums of money in the search for a potential winner. One such man was John Sanford, whose fortune was made manufacturing and selling carpets and who as a gift to his Cambridge undergraduate son Stephen, bought an ageing jumper with the appealing name of SERGEANT MURPHY. Making his fourth Grand National appearance in 1923, the thirteen-year-old used his experience of

the course to best advantage, winning by three lengths from the former winner SHAUN SPADAH and providing young Stephen Sanford with the distinction of being the first American to own a National winner. Three years later Sanford was doubly represented in the race by two of the best-fancied horses in the field, BRIGHT'S BOY and MOUNT ETNA. But the best he could achieve was third place, with BRIGHT'S BOY finishing four lengths behind JACK HORNER and OLD TAY BRIDGE. It was a fellow countryman of his, however, who led in the winner that day in 1926, the international polo player Charles Schwartz. The winning jockey

Above: Born in California, RUBIO rose from the humble occupation of pulling a hotel bus to win the 1908 Grand National at 66/1

Opposite page: Despite his journey from New Zealand being interrupted by a shipwreck, MOIFAA rose to the occasion in the finest fashion in 1904, winning by eight lengths at 25/1

Left: American-owned KELLSBORO' JACK storms clear of REALLY TRUE and SLATER to win in 1933. Although a winner many times subsequently over Aintree's fences, his lady owner never allowed him to contest the National again

Right: French contestant JIVAGO DE NEUVY and his French pilot Roget Grand cope well with Becher's on their way to finishing ninth behind HALLO DANDY in 1984

Opposite page: Racing journalist and amateur rider Marcus Armytage steers MR FRISK safely over the last fence to win the 1990 National for the American owner Mrs Lois Duffey

Below: Russian challenger GRIFEL comes to grief at Becher's first time round in the 1961 National

was Tasmanian-born Bill Watkinson. In 1928 the Maryland Hunt Cup hero BILLY BARTON looked certain to win a third National within six years for America, until falling at the final fence in that most chaotic of all races.

By the 1930s foreign competitors in the race were starting to become a regular feature and among the 42 opponents of 1931 winner GRAKLE was GYI LOVAM, owned and ridden by a Czechoslovakian cavalry officer named Captain Rudi Popler. Their long journey across Europe brought little reward, though, for after falling twice the gallant Captain called it a day.

Two more National victories followed for American owners in the thirties, before the activities of a certain Herr Hitler put the race on hold for six years. The first of these victories was provided by that outstanding Liverpool specialist KELLSBORO' JACK. American sewing machine millionaire Mr F Ambrose Clark had for many years held interests in a number of English chasers and with his seven-year-old gelding KELLSBORO' JACK entered for the 1933 Grand National, he asked his wife Florence for a £1 note. Upon receiving it, he informed his startled wife that she was now the owner of KELLSBORO' JACK. The horse duly won the race and although subsequently gaining success in a number of other Aintree chases, he was never allowed to run in the National again. Five years later it was the turn of another American lady to sample the exhilaration of winning the greatest of all races, but on that occasion the excitement proved too much for Mrs Marion du Pont Scott and she just couldn't bring herself to lead in her hero BATTLESHIP. The wife of Hollywood cowboy film star Randolph Scott, Mrs Scott retired the stallion BATTLESHIP to stud duties at her Virginia estate and in due course the horse bred the winners of five American Nationals.

Since the end of the Second World War, challengers from abroad have included GRIFEL and RELJEF from the Soviet Union in 1961, the Japanese FUJINO-O in 1966 and from the mid-1980s onwards ESSEX, FRASE and QUIRINUS from Czechoslovakia have also tested their ability without success. And, of course, the Australian champion CRISP was relegated to

second place in the very last strides of the 1973 race by RED RUM. There has also been a regular supply of French entries, which in recent years have included THE FELLOW, CIEL DE BRION and DJEDDAH. In 1991 the New Zealand-bred SEAGRAM came with a blistering late run to win the race, while another from that far-off land, LORD GYLLENE, did it rather differently in 1997, making almost all the running to win by 25 lengths.

It is still the Americans, though, who present the most realistic threat of taking steeplechasing's most prestigious trophy away from these shores. United States bred, owned and ridden, JAY TRUMP succeeded in 1965 just twelve months after TEAM SPIRIT earned his American owners a place in the winner's enclosure. Former American Ambassador Raymond Guest added the Grand National to his two Epsom Derby victories when L'ESCARGOT held on to beat RED RUM in 1975, and in 1990 Mrs Lois Duffy found her trans-Atlantic journey more than worthwhile thanks to the gelding MR FRISK.

A full 77 years after the first man from her homeland greeted his Grand National winner, SERGEANT MURPHY, Mrs Betty Moran whooped for joy when her Irish-trained PAPILLON swept past the winning post at Aintree on 8 April 2000.

Whatever the future may bring, the certainty remains that this extraordinary annual sporting contest will continue to thrill, excite and inspire the peoples of many lands, as it has since Captain Becher christened the Brook.

13

GRAND® NATIONAL

— AINTREE —

THERE CAN ONLY EVER BE ONE
certainty concerning the Grand National – the
irredeemable fact that anything can and usually
does happen. The unforeseeable pattern of that
very first Aintree contest in 1839 has persistently
been the one ingredient of the race no
contestant can plan for.

How could William McDonough have
known that his attempt on RUST would be
thwarted by a gang of rowdies preventing him
from challenging LOTTERY by blocking his way?
(If forewarned, what measures could be taken to
avoid their obstruction?) With Captain Becher,
at least his exit from the race was due merely to
his mount finding the hazards of that Brook too
severe, but yet his name has remained for ever
linked with the Grand National.

Left: 'The Winter Kings':
GRUNDON and jockey
Arthur Nightingall at
the Water Jump on
their way to victory in
the snowstorm National
of 1901

Although strangely fitting, it is surely another Aintree imponderable that a man who rode in the race just that once and without even getting round, should receive such an immortal accolade.

It is, of course, the shock winners which give this unique competition its obvious reputation for unpredictability. During the first 60 years of the Grand National such totally unfancied horses as CURE-ALL, PIONEER, ABD-EL-KADER, MISS MOWBRAY, SALAMANDER, PLAYFAIR and THE SOARER each provided the bookies with a full satchel.

Not until 1908, though, did the first really big-priced upsets begin to make studying the form of National contenders appear a complete waste of time. With RUBIO, a known victim of severe leg problems who had been reduced to pulling a hotel bus, the term 'outsider' suddenly took on a new meaning. On very heavy going and facing the stiffest test of his life against supposedly superior opposition, RUBIO gave a peerless display of jumping to stay out the trip and win comfortably by ten lengths at 66/1. In the world of horse racing it was the first major reversal of form in the twentieth century, but there would be more to follow.

With steeplechasing reaching its zenith of popularity, the prize-money for the National reached its highest level during the 1920s and with an abundance of superb jumpers available, the standard of competition for the rich prizes was equally high. Of the 42 starters for the 1928 National, no less than thirteen in the estimation of the handicapper were so superior to the remainder that they were weighted to carry

between eleven stone and twelve stone seven pounds. Only four were set with the minimum burden of ten stone, among them an almost unheard of TIPPERARY TIM. With the ditch at the Canal Turn causing untold problems after EASTER HERO toppled into it, the big field was decimated at one fell swoop and with just three runners still in the race coming to the penultimate fence, GREAT SPAN looked well able to give his young jockey Bill Payne a memorable victory. A slipped saddle at the second last, however, brought an end to their prospects, leaving American hero BILLY BARTON and everyone's no-hoper TIPPERARY TIM to decide the result. With his solitary opponent a victim at the final obstacle, TIPPERARY TIM passed the post in view of an almost silent crowd, the first 100/1 winner of the race.

The punters got a good run for their money the following year, with top weighted favourite EASTER HERO making virtually all the running at the head of his 65 rivals, until that fickle hand of fate yet again insisted on having its say. Running well within himself the gelding turned for home with only six fences left to jump, coming to Valentine's Brook with the roars of his supporters cheering him on. Upon landing over the Brook, EASTER HERO spread a plate and from there on was running almost on three legs, instinct and tremendous courage. Bravely staying on all the way to the line, EASTER HERO lost an unequal battle with GREGALACH, to finish six lengths behind the gelding to whom he was conceding seventeen pounds. For the second successive year, a 100/1 rank outsider had captured chasing's richest prize.

FORBRA and jockey Tim Hamey brought smiles to the bookmakers faces again in 1932 when, with 28 competitors failing to finish, they ran out impressive winners at 50/1, with joint favourite HEARTBREAK HILL well beaten back in sixth place.

That so dramatically close finish in 1938 had hundreds of thousands of spectators anxiously awaiting the verdict of the judge for many moments but when it was given, yet again the underdog had beaten the better fancied horse. BATTLESHIP, at 40/1, had got up on the line to defeat the popular Irish challenger ROYAL DANIELI.

In 1947 the second biggest field to face the starter lined up, 57 in all, and again the winner came from the ranks of the 'unknown'. With Britain suffering its worst winter in living memory, steeplechasing fixtures suffered enormously, with the adverse conditions forcing the abandonment of racing from mid-January until shortly before the scheduled Aintree meeting. As a result, the preparations of the majority of competing horses were severely disrupted and only a minority could be said to be anywhere near race-fit. Of these the Irish-owned, trained and ridden CAUGHOO was one, having benefited from using the beach of Sutton Strand near Dublin for his gallops. Listed with 45 others among the '100/1

others', CAUGHOO reproduced the form he had shown when winning successive Ulster Nationals, racing through the mist to win by twenty lengths from his fellow countryman LOUGH CONN. Looking all over the winner twelve months later, with just two fences left to jump the 100/1 shot ZAHIA somehow lost her way, took the wrong course and left the race at the mercy of another mare, SHEILA'S COTTAGE. Having displayed a stubborn temperament in the past, Arthur Thompson's mount was another neglected in the market, being allowed to win at the generous odds of 50/1. For the third year in a row the form book was turned upside down when RUSSIAN HERO romped home in the 1949 Grand National, totally ignored in the betting at 66/1.

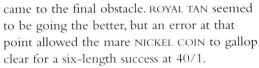

With the Festival of Britain shortly to commence on the South Bank of the Thames, 1951 began with prospects of a year of ongoing celebrations. At Aintree that spring, though, one of the most disastrous incidents in sport prompted the press to describe the great steeplechase as 'The All Fall Down National'. When the barrier rose for the start of the race, at least a third of the field were facing the wrong way, with the rest completely unprepared. In a headlong dash to make up lost ground, they reached the first fence far too fast, resulting in no less than a dozen horses coming to grief. From there on it became a catalogue of chaos, with horses tumbling or unseating their riders at almost every fence. By the time they reached the Water Jump, only five were left in the race. For those with long enough memories, it appeared a repeat of the 1928 National as only two of the 36 which started

Above: Another 100/1 shock victory for GREGALACH in 1929, with the favourite EASTER HERO in second place

Below: Considered one of the unluckiest losers of all time, Mr Anthony Mildmay on the outsider DAVY JONES in the lead at The Chair in 1936. Having made all the running, the horse ran out at the final fence with the race at his mercy

came to the final obstacle. ROYAL TAN seemed to be going the better, but an error at that point allowed the mare NICKEL COIN to gallop clear for a six-length success at 40/1.

MERRYMAN II brought a brief interlude of relief for favourite backers when winning the 1960 race as 13/2 favourite but in the next two Nationals both NICOLAUS SILVER and KILMORE were returned the winner at 28/1. Even more remote in the betting was the 1963 winner AYALA, who got up in the last 50 yards to beat CARRICKBEG, a 66/1 National triumph for young jockey Pat Buckley and trainer Keith Piggott. Fred Winter, affectionately known as 'Mr Grand National', made it two National wins as a jockey and the same as a trainer, saddling the winners JAY TRUMP in 1965 and ANGLO, a 50/1 chance twelve months later.

There was nothing minor about the shock delivered in 1967, however, when the antics of a riderless horse reduced the Grand National to what many considered utter farce. After dislodging his jockey at the first fence, a loose horse proceeded to lead the field for the remainder of the first circuit and well back on to the second, where he approached the second Becher's several lengths clear of an unusually high number of runners. Over the Brook and on to the smallest fence on the course, the jockeys were beginning to position themselves for the final stages of the race and the major part they hoped to take in it. At the very last moment before leaping for the jump, the pilotless loose horse suddenly cut to his right and cut across the oncoming runners with

catastrophic consequences. Every horse following either fell, was brought down or unseated its rider at this most innocuous of obstacles – all except one. Some way off the pace at the time, complete outsider FOINAVON was steered clear of the mêlée by his astute jockey John Buckingham and suddenly found himself alone at least 100 yards clear of the remounted pursuers. Staying on gamely, FOINAVON won by fifteen lengths from the unlucky favourite HONEY END and although the winner's starting price was returned at 100/1, those shrewd enough to have backed the horse with the totalisator were paid odds of 444/1. It is as well to remember the name of the horse which caused all the mayhem – it had to be, of course, POPHAM DOWN.

The victory of Mr Fred Pontin's SPECIFY at 28/1 in 1971 was but a minor betting upset in comparison to that of FOINAVON and with the onset of what became a domination of the race by RED RUM, the remainder of the 1970s passed without any untoward surprises. It was not until 1980, with BEN NEVIS leading home just three survivors at 40/1, that bookmakers had another better reason than usual to celebrate. With Hywel Davies conjuring a last-gasp dash from LAST SUSPECT in 1985 to score a 50/1 success, bemused punters again suffered in silence.

Since the latest modification to the fences prior to MR FRISK winning in 1990, the only rank outsider to confound the pundits by winning has been ROYAL ATHLETE in 1995 and most pundits now subscribe to the belief that the days of long-priced National winners are over.

Still, incidents such as the void race of 1993 and the postponement of 1997 sustain the evidence of the past: that anything can and very often does happen at Aintree on Grand National day.

Below: The only horse to escape the chaos at the 23rd fence in 1967, FOINAVON stays on well to beat the favourite HONEY END and RED ALLIGATOR

The MEDIA and the NATIONAL

IT IS PROBABLY superfluous to say that an event of such international acclaim as the Grand National receives colossal attention from the news agencies of the world. Yet actual live coverage of the race as we now know it has come through a long and sometimes difficult process.

Long before the present practice of newspapers including a whole sports section in their daily editions, reports of such sporting activities considered of interest were usually allowed a few paragraphs buried away in a remote column on the inner pages. In the case of the National, it was Liverpool's own paper, the *Mercury*, which supplied much of the copy concerning the early years of the race and even then, more often than not, the reports were critical and condemnatory.

Left: The BBC's special edition of the *Radio Times*, celebrating 60 years of coverage since 1927

With public interest in the steeplechase rapidly growing, however, attitudes changed among newspaper editors, with the National eventually acquiring the same importance as the Epsom Derby or Doncaster St Leger. With increased patronage from the aristocracy and finally the monarchy, the race became regularly featured in the national dailies and when the first Americans became involved towards the end of the nineteenth century, Aintree's thrilling events were read about on the other side of the Atlantic.

The rapid development of the camera brought a fascinating extension to the contents of newspapers, leading to claims by certain publishers that 'a picture can speak a thousand words'. Although this theory was small comfort to journalists, few could argue that the early grainy photographs of horses jumping Becher's Brook and The Chair did not provide an added dimension to the spectacular excitement that is the very essence of the Grand National.

Moving pictures were the wonder of the age at the start of the twentieth century and as early as 1906 a husband and wife team of cinematographers tried their hand at filming at least a small part of that year's National, which did include ASCETIC'S SILVER winning. Within two years, large portions of the race were professionally filmed and commercially displayed in 'Bioscope' cinemas throughout the country as early as 24 hours after the event. Pathé Pictorial, Movietone News and Gaumont British all jealously competed with each other over the ensuing years to bring the cinema-goer the most dramatic, exciting and incisive moving images of the Grand National. But actual live coverage of the contest as it took place still remained just a hope for the future.

That hope was realised in 1927 when the newly formed British Broadcasting Corporation relayed the first radio commentary of the race to those fortunate enough to possess a wireless. There can be no question that this was an important milestone, not just in the history of Aintree's spectacular steeplechase but equally in that of broadcasting advancement and expertise. This pioneering venture was conducted by racing journalist Meyrick Good and former Arsenal footballer George Allison and despite their task being hindered by mist hovering over the racecourse, they verbally transmitted the proceedings admirably. In 1932 the first soundtrack was included in newsreel films of the race, bringing through technology a more informative description of the event. With this breakthrough came the demand for a new breed of journalist – the racing commentator.

From the late thirties, through the forties and into the fifties, such men as Raymond Glendenning, Geoffrey Gilbey, Michael O'Hehir and Peter O'Sullevan painted a picture in words across the nation's airwaves of all the principal races – each in their own special way and each in an unhurried, perfectly modulated style, while retaining their own uniquely rich and so

recognisable accent. When it came to the National, though, there was always a special suppressed excitement in their delivery, a reverential awareness that they were recording drama at its highest level and a very special piece of sporting history.

A dispute concerning copyright ownership of the Grand National commentary led to a sadly deficient transmission in 1952, when Mrs Topham organised her own very amateur version. With wounds licked and lessons learned, the BBC complied with her wishes and they resumed their annual radio coverage of the big race in time to describe the twenty-length victory of EARLY MIST in 1953, bringing a massive sigh of relief from radio listeners.

After years of negotiations, the BBC were finally given the go-ahead to televise the big race in 1960 and with a thoroughness gained through covering the world's major sporting events, set about planning the broadcast with military style precision. Their team was by any standards a formidable one, consisting of commentators Peter O'Sullevan, Clive Graham and Peter Bromley, producers Dennis Monger, Ray Lakeland and John Vernon and very ably supported by Derek Hart and Peter Montague Evans. One of the most important features of the operation was the availability of Aintree's motor racing circuit, which was immediately identified by the production crew as a heaven sent opportunity to bring close-up images of the action into viewer's homes. Using a mobile camera mounted on a motor car travelling alongside the competitors, it provided tremendous scope to capture all the action and excitement of the event as it happened, in a manner never before envisaged. What, in today's high-tech world may appear to have been a simple task, was 40 years ago an enormous step into the unknown and one which was to test the ability and professionalism of all concerned with the project.

With infinite attention to detail, a group of men totally committed to their calling brilliantly conveyed to millions of television viewers the athleticism, courage and intensity of spirit required to win the Grand National. That first televised coverage of Aintree's historic marathon inspired all associated with it to continue with even greater zest, in depicting an event guaranteed to sieze the imagination of those watching and in so doing make them realise they were watching genuine sportmanship, in the raw and true endeavour as it should always be demonstrated.

A further dimension was added to the screening of the race in 1969 when colour filming was introduced by the BBC and at the end of the transmission, winning jockey Eddie Harty provided presenter David Coleman with a rapid-fire description of his victory.

In 1985 the ultra-cool Desmond Lynam brought a relaxed, friendly and reassuring bearing to one of the most demanding jobs in the media. Quickly entering into the spirit of the occasion, he increased the demands on his talents by running his own horse ANOTHER

DUKE twelve months later. Yet far and away the most respected, admired and professional of them all, Peter O'Sullevan bade a fond farewell to an incredible 50 years of superb Grand National commentaries in that anxious year of 1997. As true as when first spoken, nobody did it better.

ART and the NATIONAL

15

GRAND®
NATIONAL
— AINTREE —

IT IS HARDLY SURPRISING

that over the years a contest as action-packed as the Grand National has presented artists with hugely appealing opportunities to depict a vast variety of thrilling scenes.

One of the most famous attempts to recreate specific incidents of Liverpool's most famous equestrian contest are the engravings by J Harris after the illustrations of Francis Calcraft Turner, showing activities during the first Great Liverpool Steeplechase in 1839. In four separate prints the contestants are first shown preparing to line up for the start, Captain Becher clambering from the Brook, the infamous Stone Wall and the finish of the race with LOTTERY beating SEVENTY FOUR and PAULINA.

Left: Peter Curling's dramatic painting of the runners at The Chair in the 1991 Grand National. Eventual winner SEAGRAM is number 11 in the centre of the field

It is interesting to note that the sketch of Becher at Aintree's best known obstacle was used on the cover of the Liverpool race card up until 1976. No less a distinguished artist than John Frederick Herring subsequently produced an oil painting of LOTTERY, at a time when such practices were reserved almost exclusively for Derby or St Leger winners.

William Tasker's wonderful oil painting of the Stone Wall in 1843 belongs to the estate of the American millionaire racehorse owner Paul

Mellon and displays in the most dramatic fashion the severity of the obstacle, together with the exceptional demands made on both horses and riders especially at that time in history. With typical generosity, Mr Mellon shipped the huge painting over to this country in 1989 to take its place in the Grand National Exhibition at The County Museum in Liverpool.

The first written work published on the race in 1907 was *Heroes and Heroines of the Grand National* by George Finch Mason, a man obviously multi-talented for in addition to producing a chronicle of Aintree's affairs from the very start, he also illustrated it with many lively scenes. Among his most popular works was his view of the snowstorm race of 1901, showing eventual winner GRUDON leading DRUMCREE and BUFFALO BILL at the Water jump.

In due course that Christmas-like scene became inspiration for a very fine equestrian artist signing himself 'Snaffles', who was in actuality Charlie Johnson Payne. His painting, entitled *The Worst View in Europe*, showing a lone horse and rider approaching Becher's Brook during a raging blizzard, has been reproduced as a print many times and is even now available in the form of a greeting card. 'Snaffles' was a regular visitor to the Grand National, along with such other excellent artists as Lionel Edwards, Cecil Aldin and Gilbert Holiday and although each had their own individual style, their work shared a common exuberance and vitality. With all the colour, action and urgency of the occasion literally jumping out of their pictures, it is so very evident that these men experienced at first hand the atmosphere and fascination of the moment.

As a salute to the BBC's first televised National in 1960, *The Sporting Life* commissioned a painting to be reproduced in their broadsheet on the big day and their chosen artist, Lionel Edwards, delivered a magnificent scene of the always popular WYNDBURGH jumping Becher's Brook in splendid style. Peter Biegel was a protégé of this artist who quickly gained a reputation to match that of his teacher, his action-packed scenes of the pile-up at the Canal Turn in 1929 and the chaos of FOINAVON's year ranking high among his superb works. Others influenced by the Grand National as a

means of demonstrating their outstanding artistic talent include Lynwood Palmer, Sir Alfred Munnings, Charles Simpson, TP Earl and GD Giles. The example they provided set the standard for racing art of the future.

In more recent times the work of Michael Lyne has greatly added to the faithful artistic translation of National incidents, allowing a feeling of closeness to the action rarely obtainable, even through the eye of a roving television camera.

The importance of art in reporting Aintree's famous event was suitably acknowledged by Aintree Racecourse Company in 1991 when they organised an art competition with that year's race as the theme. The overall winner was Peter Curling, who submitted a vigorous picture of the runners galloping towards the mighty Chair with its gaping ditch. Capturing all the tension, concentration and resolution which is as much a part of the Grand National as Becher's Brook itself, the artist's excellent painting holds a permanent and prominent position on the wall of Aintree's Martell Suite.

With such fine craftsmen as Peter Curling, Neil Cawthorne, Adrian and David Dent and, of course, not forgetting those extremely talented women Margaret Barrett, Claire Burton and Amanda Gooseman, the long tradition is in

Left: A favourite meeting place these days for visitors to Aintree, Philip Blacker's wonderful testament to courage, the RED RUM statue

very safe hands and they and their predecessors have served their craft excellently.

Jockey turned sculptor Philip Blacker has also excelled in his chosen medium and his now famous RED RUM statue proudly overlooks the scene of the horse's greatest triumphs.

Below: TROYTOWN leading at Valentine's Brook during the 1920 National as viewed by Cecil Aldin

RACE RESULTS

1839

1st	LOTTERY	(Jem Mason)	5/1 Fav.
2nd	SEVENTY FOUR	(Tom Olliver)	
3rd	PAULINA	(Mr Martin)	
4th	TRUE BLUE	(Mr Barker)	
	17 ran; 7 finished		

1840

1st	JERRY	(Mr Bretherton)	12/1
2nd	ARTHUR	(Mr A. McDonough)	8/1 (remounted)
3rd	VALENTINE	(Mr A. Power)	n/q
4th	THE SEA	(Marquis of Waterford)	n/q
	12 ran; 4 finished		

1841

1st	CHARITY	(Mr Powell)	14/1
2nd	CIGAR	(Mr A.McDonough)	4/1
3rd	PETER SIMPLE	(Walker)	6/1
4th	REVEALER	(Mr Barker)	n/q
	11 ran; 7 finished		

1842

1st	GAY LAD	(Tom Olliver)	7/1
2nd	SEVENTY FOUR	(Powell)	6/1
3rd	PETER SIMPLE	(Mr Hunter)	6/1 (remounted)
4th	THE RETURNED	(Mr W.Hope-Johnstone)	15/1
	15 ran; 5 finished		

1843

1st	VANGUARD	(Tom Olliver)	12/1
2nd	NIMROD	(Scott)	10/1
3rd	DRAGSMAN	(Mr Crickmere)	10/1
4th	CLAUDE DUVAL	(Tomblin)	n/q
	16 ran; 9 finished		

1844

1st	DISCOUNT	(Mr Crickmere)	5/1 Jnt/Fav.
2nd	THE RETURNED	(Scott)	15/1
3rd	TOM TUG	(Rackley)	n/q
4th	CAESAR	(Barker)	n/q
	15 ran; 9 finished		

1845

1st	CURE-ALL	(Mr W.J.Loft)	n/q
2nd	PETER SIMPLE	(Frisby)	9/1
3rd	THE EXQUISITE	(L Byrne)	n/q
4th	TOM TUG	(Mr Crickmere)	5/1
	15 ran; 4 finished		

1846

1st	PIONEER	(W.Taylor)	n/q
2nd	CULVERTHORPE	(Rackley)	12/1
3rd	SWITCHER	(D.Wynne)	n/q
4th	FIREFLY	(L.Byrne)	7/1
	22 ran; 5 finished		

1847

1st	MATTHEW	(D.Wynne)	10/1 Jnt/Fav.
2nd	ST LEGER	(Tom Olliver)	15/1
3rd	JERRY	(Bradley)	100/8
4th	PIONEER	(Captain Peel)	15/1
	26 ran; 6 finished		

1848

1st	CHANDLER	(Captain J.L.Little)	12/1
2nd	THE CURATE	(Tom Olliver)	6/1 Fav.
3rd	BRITISH YEOMAN	(Mr Bevill)	n/q
4th	STANDARD GUARD	(Taylor)	100/6
	29 ran; 4 finished		

1849

1st	PETER SIMPLE	(T.Cunningham)	20/1
2nd	THE KNIGHT OF GWYNNE	(Captain D'Arcy)	8/1
3rd	PRINCE GEORGE	(Tom Olliver)	5/1 Fav.
4th	ALFRED	(D.Wynne)	12/1
	24 ran; 6 finished		

1850

1st	ABD-EL-KADER	(C.Green)	n/q
2nd	THE KNIGHT OF GWYNNE	(D.Wynne)	12/1
3rd	SIR JOHN	(J.Ryan)	7/1
4th	TIPPERARY BOY	(S.Darling)	n/q
	32 ran; 7 finished		

1851

1st	ABD-EL-KADER	(T.Abbot)	7/1
2nd	MARIA DAY	(J.Frisby)	100/6
3rd	SIR JOHN	(J.Ryan)	7/1
4th	HALF-AND-HALF	(R.Sly, jnr)	20/1
	21 ran; 10 finished		

1852

1st	MISS MOWBRAY	(Mr A.Goodman)	n/q
2nd	MAURICE DALEY	(C.Boyce)	n/q
3rd	SIR PETER LAURIE	(W.Holman)	30/1
4th	CHIEFTAIN	(Harrison)	10/1
	24 ran; 7 finished		

1853

1st	PETER SIMPLE	(Tom Olliver)	9/1
2nd	MISS MOWBRAY	(Mr F.Gordon)	5/1 Fav.
3rd	OSCAR	(Mr A.Goodman)	6/1
4th	SIR PETER LAURIE	(W.Holman)	12/1
	21 ran; 7 finished		

1854

1st	BOURTON	(J.Tasker)	4/1 Fav.
2nd	SPRING	(W.Archer)	20/1
3rd	CRABBS	(D.Wynne)	10/1
4th	MALEY	(Thrift)	50/1
	20 ran; 7 finished		

1855

1st	WANDERER	(J.Hanlon)	25/1
2nd	FREETRADER	(Meaney)	50/1
3rd	MAURICE DALEY	(R.James)	20/1
4th	JANUS	(H.Lamplugh)	33/1
	20 ran; 7 finished		

1856

1st	FREETRADER	(G.Stevens)	25/1
2nd	MINERVA	(R.Sly, jnr)	25/1
3rd	MINOS	(R.James)	n/q
4th	HOPELESS STAR	(W.White)	25/1
	21 ran; 6 finished		

1857

1st	EMIGRANT	(C.Boyce)	10/1
2nd	WEATHERCOCK	(C.Green)	25/1
3rd	TREACHERY	(Poole)	n/q
4th	WESTMINSTER	(Palmer)	n/q
	28 ran; 8 finished		

1858

1st	LITTLE CHARLEY	(W.Archer)	100/6
2nd	WEATHERCOCK	(Mr Edwards)	25/1
3rd	XANTHUS	(F.Balchin)	33/1
4th	MORGAN RATTLER	(T.Burrows)	100/6
	16 ran; 5 finished		

1859

1st	HALF CASTE	(C.Green)	7/1
2nd	JEAN DU QUESNE	(H.Lamplugh)	10/1
3rd	HUNTSMAN	(B.Land,jnr)	100/8
4th	MIDGE	(D.Meaney)	33/1
	20 ran; 8 finished		

1860

1st	ANATIS	(Mr Thomas)	7/2 Fav.
2nd	HUNTSMAN	(Captain T.M.Townley)	33/1
3rd	XANTHUS	(F.Balchin)	10/1
4th	MARIA AGNES	(G.Stevens)	10/1
	19 ran; 7 finished		

1861

1st	JEALOUSY	(J.Kendall)	5/1
2nd	THE DANE	(W.White)	33/1
3rd	OLD BEN ROE	(G.Waddington)	10/1
4th	BRIDEGROOM	(Mr FitzAdam)	25/1
	24 ran; 5 finished		

1862

1st	HUNTSMAN	(H.Lamplugh)	3/1 Fav.
2nd	BRIDEGROOM	(B.Land, jnr)	10/1
3rd	ROMEO	(Mr C.Bennett)	100/8
4th	XANTHUS	(R.Sherrard)	25/1
	13 ran; 5 finished		

1863

1st	EMBLEM	(G.Stevens)	4/1
2nd	ARBURY	(Mr A.Goodman)	25/1
3rd	YALLER GAL	(Mr Dixon)	20/1
4th	FOSCO	(Mr G.Holman)	40/1
	16 ran; 6 finished		

1864

1st	EMBLEMATIC	(G.Stevens)	10/1
2nd	ARBURY	(B.Land,jnr)	40/1
3rd	CHESTER	(W.White)	40/1
4th	THOMASTOWN	(J.Murphy)	33/1
	25 ran; 5 finished		

1865

1st	ALCIBIADE	(Captain H.Coventry)	100/7
2nd	HALL COURT	(Captain A.C.Tempest)	50/1
3rd	EMBLEMATIC	(G.Stevens)	5/1 Fav.
4th	MISTAKE	(Jarvis)	n/q
	23 ran; 6 finished		

1866

1st	SALAMANDER	(Mr A.Goodman)	40/1
2nd	CORTOLVIN	(J.Page)	8/1
3rd	CREOLE	(G.Waddington)	15/1
4th	LIGHTHEART	(E.Jones)	50/1
	30 ran; 5 finished		

1867

1st	CORTOLVIN	(J.Page)	16/1
2nd	FAN	(Thorpe)	9/1
3rd	SHANGARRY	(Mr Thomas)	14/1
4th	GLOBULE	(G.Holman)	14/1
	23 ran; 10 finished		

1868

1st	THE LAMB	(Mr Edwards)	9/1
2nd	PEARL DIVER	(Tomlinson)	10/1
3rd	ALCIBIADE	(Colonel G.W.Knox)	16/1
4th	CAPTAIN CROSSTREE	(W.Reeves)	33/1
	21 ran; 7 finished		

1869

1st	THE COLONEL	(G.Stevens)	100/7
2nd	HALL COURT	(Captain A.C.Tempest)	100/1
3rd	GARDENER	(Ryan)	1000/15
4th	ALCIBIADE	(Colonel G.W.Knox)	20/1
	22 ran; 9 finished		

1870

1st	THE COLONEL	(G.Stevens)	7/2 Fav.
2nd	THE DOCTOR	(G.Holman)	5/1
3rd	PRIMROSE	(Mr W.R.Brockton)	10/1
4th	SURNEY	(R.I'Anson)	100/8
	23 ran; 8 finished		

1871

1st	THE LAMB	(Mr Thomas)	11/2
2nd	DESPATCH	(G.Waddington)	10/1
3rd	SCARRINGTON	(Cranshaw)	100/1
4th	PEARL DIVER	(J.Page)	4/1 Fav.
25 ran; 8 finished			

1872

1st	CASSE TETE	(J.Page)	20/1
2nd	SCARRINGTON	(R.I'Anson)	100/6
3rd	DESPATCH	(G.Waddington)	100/30 Fav.
4th	THE LAMB	(Mr Thomas)	100/8
25 ran; 9 finished			

1873

1st	DISTURBANCE	(Mr J.M.Richardson)	20/1
2nd	RYSHWORTH	(Boxall)	15/2
3rd	COLUMBINE	(Harding)	n/q
4th	MASTER MOWBRAY	(G.Holman)	12/1
28 ran; 6 finished			

1874

1st	REUGNY	(Mr J.M.Richardson)	5/1Fav.
2nd	CHIMNEY SWEEP	(J.Jones)	25/1
3rd	MERLIN	(J.Adams)	40/1
4th	DEFENCE	(Mr Rolly)	33/1
22 ran; 8 finished			

1875

1st	PATHFINDER	(Mr Thomas)	100/6
2nd	DAINTY	(Mr Hathaway)	25/1
3rd	LA VEINE	(J.Page)	6/1 Fav.
4th	JACKAL	(R.Marsh)	7/1
19 ran; 8 finished			

1876

1st	REGAL	(J.Cannon)	25/1
2nd	CONGRESS	(Mr E.P.Wilson)	25/1
3rd	SHIFNAL	(R.I'Anson)	25/1
4th	CHIMNEY SWEEP	(J.Jones)	25/1
19 ran; 7 finished			

1877

1st	AUSTERLITZ	(Mr F.G.Hobson)	15/1
2nd	CONGRESS	(J.Cannon)	20/1
3rd	THE LIBERATOR	(Mr Thomas)	25/1
4th	CHIMNEY SWEEP	(J.Jones)	7/1
16 ran; 7 finished			

1878

1st	SHIFNAL	(J.Jones)	7/1
2nd	MARTHA	(Mr T.Beasley)	20/1
3rd	PRIDE OF KILDARE	(Mr G.Moore)	6/1
4th	JACKAL	(Jewitt)	100/8
12 ran; 7 finished			

1879

1st	THE LIBERATOR	(Mr G.Moore)	5/1
2nd	JACKAL	(J.Jones)	1000/65
3rd	MARTHA	(Mr T.Beasley)	50/1
4th	WILD MONARCH	(Andrews)	20/1
18 ran; 10 finished			

1880

1st	EMPRESS	(Mr T.Beasley)	8/1
2nd	THE LIBERATOR	(Mr G.Moore)	11/2
3rd	DOWNPATRICK	(P.Gavin)	100/15
4th	JUPITER TONANS	(Mr J.F.Lee–Barber)	50/1
14 ran; 10 finished			

1881

1st	WOODBROOK	(Mr T.Beasley)	11/2 Jnt/Fav.
2nd	REGAL	(J.Jewitt)	11/1
3rd	THORNFIELD	(R.Marsh)	11/2 Jnt/Fav.
4th	NEW GLASGOW	(Captain A.J.Smith)	100/8
13 ran; 9 finished			

1882

1st	SEAMAN	(Lord Manners)	10/1
2nd	CYRUS	(Mr T.Beasley)	9/2
3rd	ZOEDONE	(Captain A.J.Smith)	25/1
Only three completed the course			
12 ran; 3 finished			

1883

1st	ZOEDONE	(Count C.Kinsky)	100/7
2nd	BLACK PRINCE	(D.Canavan)	33/1
3rd	MOHICAN	(Mr H.Beasley)	9/1
4th	DOWNPATRICK	(Mr T.Widger)	100/7
10 ran; 7 finished			

1884

1st	VOLUPTUARY	(Mr E.P.Wilson)	10/1
2nd	FRIGATE	(Mr H.Beasley)	10/1
3rd	ROQUEFORT	(J.Childs)	10/1
4th	CYRUS	(J.Jewitt)	9/1
15 ran; 6 finished			

1885

1st	ROQUEFORT	(Mr E.P.Wilson)	100/30 Fav.
2nd	FRIGATE	(Mr H.Beasley)	7/1
3rd	BLACK PRINCE	(T.Skelton)	33/1
4th	REDPATH	(Mr A.Coventry)	20/1
19 ran; 9 finished			

1886

1st	OLD JOE	(T.Skelton)	25/1
2nd	TOO GOOD	(Mr H.Beasley)	7/1
3rd	GAMECOCK	(W.E.Stephens)	50/1
4th	MAGPIE	(Mr W.Woodland)	200/1
23 ran; 8 finished			

1887

1st	GAMECOCK	(W.Daniels)	20/1
2nd	SAVOYARD	(T.Skelton)	100/14
3rd	JOHNNY LONGTAIL	(J.Childs)	40/1
4th	CHANCELLOR	(Mr W.H.Moore)	20/1
16 ran; 6 finished			

1888

1st	PLAYFAIR	(G.Mawson)	40/1
2nd	FRIGATE	(Mr W.Beasley)	100/9
3rd	BALLOT BOX	(W.Nightingall)	25/1
4th	RINGLET	(T.Skelton)	100/9
20 ran; 9 finished			

1889

1st	FRIGATE	(Mr T.Beasley)	8/1
2nd	WHY NOT	(Mr C.J.Cunningham)	11/1
3rd	M.P.	(A.Nightingall)	20/1
4th	BELLONA	(Mr C.W.Waller)	20/1
20 ran; 10 finished			

1890

1st	ILEX	(A.Nightngall)	4/1 Fav.
2nd	PAN	(W.Halsey)	100/1
3rd	M.P.	(Mr W.H.Moore)	8/1
4th	BRUNSWICK	(G.Mawson)	100/1
16 ran; 6 finished			

1891

1st	COME AWAY	(Mr H.Beasley)	4/1 Fav.
2nd	CLOISTER	(Captain E.R.Owen)	20/1
3rd	ILEX	(A.Nightingall)	5/1
4th	ROQUEFORT	(F.Guy)	40/1
21 ran; 6 finished			

1892

1st	FATHER O'FLYNN	(Capt.E.R.Owen)	20/1
2nd	CLOISTER	(Mr J.C.Dormer)	11/2 Fav.
3rd	ILEX	(A.Nightingall)	20/1
4th	ARDCARN	(T.Kavanagh)	10/1
25 ran; 11 finished			

1893

1st	CLOISTER	(W.Dollery)	9/2 Fav.
2nd	AESOP	(A.H.Barker)	100/12
3rd	WHY NOT	(A.Nightingall)	5/1
4th	TIT FOR TAT	(G.Williamson)	25/1
15 ran; 8 finished			

1894

1st	WHY NOT	(A.Nightingall)	5/1 Jnt/Fav.
2nd	LADY ELLEN II	(T.Kavanagh)	25/1
3rd	WILD MAN FROM BORNEO	(Mr J.Widger)	40/1
4th	TROUVILLE	(Mr J.C.Cheney)	25/1
14 ran; 9 finished			

1895

1st	WILD MAN FROM BORNEO	(Mr J.Widger)	10/1
2nd	CATHAL	(H.Escott)	100/8
3rd	VAN DER BERG	(W.Dollery)	25/1
4th	MANIFESTO	(T.Kavanagh)	100/8
19 ran; 11 finished			

1896

1st	THE SOARER	(Mr D.G.M.Campbell)	40/1
2nd	FATHER O'FLYNN	(Mr C.Grenfell)	40/1
3rd	BISCUIT	(E.Matthews)	25/1
4th	BARCALWHEY	(C.Hogan)	1000/30
28 ran; 9 finished			

1897

1st	MANIFESTO	(T.Kavanagh)	6/1 Fav.
2nd	FILBERT	(Mr C.Beatty)	100/1
3rd	FORD OF FYNE	(Mr F.Withington)	25/1
4th	PRINCE ALBERT	(Mr G.S.Davies)	25/1
28 ran; 10 finished			

1898

1st	DROGHEDA	(J.Gourley)	25/1
2nd	CATHAL	(Mr R.Ward)	7/1
3rd	GAUNTLET	(W.Taylor)	100/12
4th	FILBERT	(Mr C.Beatty)	25/1
25 ran; 10 finished			

1899

1st	MANIFESTO	(G.Williamson)	5/1
2nd	FORD OF FYNE	(E.Matthews)	40/1
3rd	ELLIMAN	(E.Piggott)	20/1
4th	DEAD LEVEL	(F.Mason)	33/1
19 ran; 11 finished			

1900

1st	AMBUSH II	(A.Anthony)	4/1
2nd	BARSAC	(W.Halsey)	25/1
3rd	MANIFESTO	(G.Williamson)	6/1
4th	BREEMOUNTS PRIDE	(Mr G.S.Davies)	20/1
16 ran; 11 finished			

1901

1st	GRUDON	(A.Nightingall)	9/1
2nd	DRUMCREE	(Mr H.Nugent)	10/1
3rd	BUFFALO BILL	(H.Taylor)	33/1
4th	LEVANTER	(F.Mason)	5/1 Fav.
24 ran; 9 finished			

1902

1st	SHANNON LASS	(D.Read)	20/1
2nd	MATTHEW	(W.Morgan)	50/1
3rd	MANIFESTO	(E.Piggott)	100/6
4th	DETAIL	(A.Nightingall)	25/1
21 ran; 11 finished			

1903

1st	DRUMCREE	(P.Woodland)	13/2 Fav.
2nd	DETAIL	(A.Nightingall)	100/14
3rd	MANIFESTO	(G.Williamson)	25/1
4th	KIRKLAND	(F.Mason)	100/8
23 ran; 7 finished			

1904

1st	MOIFAA	(A.Birch)	25/1
2nd	KIRKLAND	(F.Mason)	100/7
3rd	THE GUNNER	(Mr J.W.Widger)	25/1
4th	SHAUN ABOO	(A.Waddington)	n/q
26 ran; 8 finished			

1905

1st	KIRKLAND	(F.Mason)	6/1
2nd	NAPPER TANDY	(P.Woodland)	25/1
3rd	BUCKAWAY II	(A.Newey)	100/1
4th	RANUNCULUS	(C.Hollebone)	7/1
27 ran; 7 finished			

1906

1st	ASCETIC'S SILVER	(Mr A.Hastings)	20/1
2nd	RED LAD	(C.Kelly)	33/1
3rd	AUNT MAY	(Mr H.S.Persse)	25/1
4th	CRAUTACAUN	(I.Anthony)	100/6
23 ran; 9 finished			

1907

1st	EREMON	(A.Newey)	8/1
2nd	TOM WEST	(H.Murphy)	100/6
3rd	PATLANDER	(J.Lynn)	n/q
4th	RAVENSCLIFFE	(F.Lyall)	100/7
	23 ran; 8 finished		

1908

1st	RUBIO	(H.B.Bletsoe)	66/1
2nd	MATTIE MACGREGOR	(W.Bissill)	25/1
3rd	THE LAWYER III	(Mr P.Whitaker)	100/7
4th	FLAXMAN	(A.Anthony)	33/1
	24 ran; 8 finished		

1909

1st	LUTTEUR III	(G.Parfrement)	100/9 Jnt/Fav.
2nd	JUDAS	(R.Chadwick)	33/1
3rd	CAUBEEN	(F.Mason)	20/1
4th	TOM WEST	(H.Murphy)	100/6
	32 ran; 16 finished		

1910

1st	JENKINSTOWN	(R.Chadwick)	100/8
2nd	JERRY M	(E.Driscoll)	6/1 Fav.
3rd	ODOR	(Mr R.H.Hall)	n/q
4th	CARSEY	(E.R.Morgan)	100/8
	25 ran; 5 finished		

1911

1st	GLENSIDE	(Mr.J.R.Anthony)	20/1
2nd	RATHNALLY	(R.Chadwick)	8/1 (remounted)
3rd	SHADY GIRL	(G.Clancy)	33/1 (remounted)
4th	FOOL-HARDY	(Mr W.Macneill)	50/1 (remounted)
	26 ran; 4 finished		

1912

1st	JERRY M	(E.Piggott)	4/1 Jnt/Fav.
2nd	BLOODSTONE	(F.Lyall)	40/1
3rd	AXLE PIN	(I.Anthony)	20/1
4th	CARSEY	(Mr H.W.Tyrwhitt-Drake)	100/8
	24 ran; 7 finished		

1913

1st	COVERTCOAT	(P.Woodland)	100/9
2nd	IRISH MAIL	(O.Anthony)	25/1
3rd	CARSEY	(Mr H.W.Tyrwhitt-Drake)	100/9 (remounted)
	★Only three completed the course★		
	22 ran; 3 finished		

1914

1st	SUNLOCH	(W.J.Smith)	100/6
2nd	TRIANON III	(C.Hawkins)	100/8
3rd	LUTTEUR III	(A.Carter)	10/1
4th	RORY O'MOORE	(Mr P.Whitaker)	20/1
	20 ran; 4 finished		

1915

1st	ALLY SLOPER	(Mr J.R.Anthony)	100/8
2nd	JACOBUS	(A.Newey)	25/1
3rd	FATHER CONFESSOR	(A.Aylin)	10/1
4th	ALFRED NOBLE	(T.Hulme)	25/1
	20 ran; 5 finished		

1919

1st	POETHLYN	(E.Piggott)	11/4 Fav.
2nd	BALLYBOGGAN	(W.Head)	9/1
3rd	POLLEN	(A.Escott)	100/7
4th	LOCH ALLEN	(J.Kelly)	33/1
	22 ran; 7 finished		

1920

1st	TROYTOWN	(Mr J.R.Anthony)	6/1
2nd	THE TURK II	(R.Burford)	n/q
3rd	THE BORE	(Mr H.A.Brown)	28/1
4th	SERGEANT MURPHY	(W.Smith)	100/7
	24 ran; 5 finished		

1921

1st	SHAUN SPADAH	(F.B.Rees)	100/9
2nd	THE BORE	(Mr H.A.Brown)	9/1 Fav. (remounted)
3rd	ALL WHITE	(R.Chadwick)	30/1 (remounted)
4th	TURKEY BUZZARD	(Capt.G.H.Bennet)	100/9 (remounted)
	35 ran; 4 finished		

1922

1st	MUSIC HALL	(L.B.Rees)	100/9
2nd	DRIFTER	(W.Watkinson)	18/1
3rd	TAFFYTUS	(T.E.Leader)	66/1
4th	SERGEANT MURPHY	(C.Hawkins)	100/6 (remounted)
	32 ran; 5 finished		

1923

1st	SERGEANT MURPHY	(Capt.G.H.Bennet)	100/6
2nd	SHAUN SPADAH	(F.B.Rees)	20/1
3rd	CONJURER II	(Mr C.P.Dewhurst)	100/6
4th	PUNT GUN	(M.Tighe)	20/1
	28 ran; 7 finished		

1924

1st	MASTER ROBERT	(R.Trudgill)	25/1
2nd	FLY MASK	(J.Moylan)	100/7
3rd	SILVO	(G.Goswell)	100/7
4th	DRIFTER	(G.Calder)	40/1
	30 ran; 8 finished		

1925

1st	DOUBLE CHANCE	(Major J.P.Wilson)	100/9
2nd	OLD TAY BRIDGE	(J.R.Anthony)	9/1 Fav.
3rd	FLY MASK	(E.Doyle)	10/1
4th	SPRIG	(T.E.Leader)	33/1
	33 ran; 10 finished		

1926

1st	JACK HORNER	(W.Watkinson)	25/1
2nd	OLD TAY BRIDGE	(J.R.Anthony)	8/1
3rd	BRIGHT'S BOY	(E.Doyle)	25/1
4th	SPRIG	(T.E.Leader)	5/1 Fav.
	30 ran; 13 finished		

1927

1st	SPRIG	(T.E.Leader)	8/1 Fav.
2nd	BOVRIL III	(Mr G.W.Pennington)	100/1
3rd	BRIGHT'S BOY	(J.R.Anthony)	100/7
4th	DRINMOND	(Mr J.B.Balding)	66/1
	37 ran; 7 finished		

1928

1st	TIPPERARY TIM	(Mr W.P.Dutton)	100/1
2nd	BILLY BARTON	(T.B.Cullinan)	33/1 (remounted)
Only two completed the course			
42 ran; 2 finished			

1929

1st	GREGALACH	(R.Everett)	100/1
2nd	EASTER HERO	(J.Moloney)	9/1 Fav.
3rd	RICHMOND II	(W.Stott)	40/1
4th	MELLERAY'S BELLE	(J.Mason)	200/1
66 ran; 10 finished			

1930

1st	SHAUN GOILIN	(T.B.Cullinan)	100/8
2nd	MELLERAY'S BELLE	(J.Mason)	20/1
3rd	SIR LINDSAY	(D.Williams)	100/7
4th	GLANGESIA	(J.Browne)	33/1
41 ran; 6 finished			

1931

1st	GRAKLE	(R.Lyall)	100/6
2nd	GREGALACH	(J.Moloney)	25/1
3rd	ANNANDALE	(T.Morgan)	100/1
4th	RHYTICERE	(L.Niaudot)	50/1
43 ran; 9 finished			

1932

1st	FORBRA	(J.Hamey)	50/1
2nd	EGREMONT	(Mr E.C.Paget)	33/1
3rd	SHAUN GOILIN	(D.Williams)	40/1
4th	NEAR EAST	(T.McCarthy)	50/1
36 ran; 8 finished			

1933

1st	KELLSBORO' JACK	(D.Williams)	25/1
2nd	REALLY TRUE	(Mr F.Furlong)	66/1
3rd	SLATER	(Mr M.Barry)	50/1
4th	DELANEIGE	(J.Moloney)	20/1
34 ran; 19 finished			

1934

1st	GOLDEN MILLER	(G.Wilson)	8/1
2nd	DELANEIGE	(J.Moloney)	100/7
3rd	THOMOND II	(W.Speck)	18/1
4th	FORBRA	(G.Hardy)	100/8
30 ran; 8 finished			

1935

1st	REYNOLDSTOWN	(Mr F.Furlong)	22/1
2nd	BLUE PRINCE	(W.Parvin)	40/1
3rd	THOMOND II	(W.Speck)	9/2
4th	LAZY BOOTS	(G.Owen)	100/1
27 ran; 6 finished			

1936

1st	REYNOLDSTOWN	(Mr F.Walwyn)	10/1
2nd	EGO	(Mr H.Llewellyn)	50/1
3rd	BACHELOR PRINCE	(J.Fawcus)	66/1
4th	CROWN PRINCE	(Mr R.Strutt)	66/1
35 ran; 10 finished			

1937

1st	ROYAL MAIL	(E.Williams)	100/6
2nd	COOLEEN	(J.Fawcus)	33/1
3rd	PUCKA BELLE	(Mr E.W.W.Bailey)	100/6
4th	EGO	(Mr H.L.Lewellyn)	10/1
33 ran; 7 finished			

ROYAL MAIL

1938

1st	BATTLESHIP	(B.Hobbs)	40/1
2nd	ROYAL DANIELI	(D.Moore)	18/1
3rd	WORKMAN	(J.Brogan)	28/1
4th	COOLEEN	(J.Fawcus)	8/1 Jnt/Fav.
36 ran; 13 finished			

1939

1st	WORKMAN	(T.Hyde)	100/8
2nd	MACMOFFAT	(I.Alder)	25/1
3rd	KILSTAR	(G.Archibald)	8/1 Fav.
4th	COOLEEN	(J.Fawcus)	22/1
37 ran; 11 finished			

1940

1st	BOGSKAR	(M.A.Jones)	25/1
2nd	MACMOFFAT	(I.Alder)	8/1
3rd	GOLD ARROW	(P.Lay)	50/1
4th	SYMAETHIS	(M.Feakes)	100/6
30 ran; 17 finished			

1946

1st	LOVELY COTTAGE	(Capt.R.Petre)	25/1
2nd	JACK FINLAY	(W.Kidney)	100/1
3rd	PRINCE REGENT	(T.Hyde)	3/1 Fav.
4th	HOUSEWARMER	(A.Brabazon)	100/1
34 ran; 6 finished			

1947

1st	CAUGHOO	(E.Dempsey)	100/1
2nd	LOUGH CONN	(D.McCann)	33/1
3rd	KAMI	(Mr J.Hislop)	33/1
4th	PRINCE REGENT	(T.Hyde)	8/1 Fav.
57 ran; 21 finished			

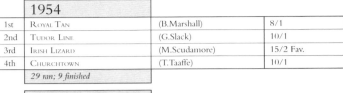

1948

1st	SHEILA'S COTTAGE	(A.P.Thompson)	50/1
2nd	FIRST OF THE DANDIES	(J.Brogan)	25/1
3rd	CROMWELL	(Lord Mildmay)	33/1
4th	HAPPY HOME	(G.Kelly)	33/1
	43 ran; 14 finished		

1949

1st	RUSSIAN HERO	(L.McMorrow)	66/1
2nd	ROIMOND	(R.Francis)	22/1
3rd	ROYAL MOUNT	(P.J.Doyle)	18/1
4th	CROMWELL	(Lord Mildmay)	6/1 Fav.
	43 ran; 11 finished		

1954

1st	ROYAL TAN	(B.Marshall)	8/1
2nd	TUDOR LINE	(G.Slack)	10/1
3rd	IRISH LIZARD	(M.Scudamore)	15/2 Fav.
4th	CHURCHTOWN	(T.Taaffe)	10/1
	29 ran; 9 finished		

1955

1st	QUARE TIMES	(P.Taaffe)	100/9
2nd	TUDOR LINE	(G.Slack)	10/1
3rd	CAREY'S COTTAGE	(T.Taaffe)	20/1
4th	GIGOLO	(R.Curran)	100/6
	30 ran; 13 finished		

RUSSIAN HERO

QUARE TIMES

1950

1st	FREEBOOTER	(J.Power)	10/1 Jnt/Fav.
2nd	WOT NO SUN	(A.P.Thompson)	100/7
3rd	ACTHON MAJOR	(R.J.O'Ryan)	33/1
4th	ROWLAND ROY	(R.Black)	40/1
	49 ran; 7 finished		

1951

1st	NICKEL COIN	(J.A.Bullock)	40/1
2nd	ROYAL TAN	(Mr A.S.O'Brien)	22/1
3rd	DERRINSTOWN	(A.Power)	66/1 (remounted)
	Only three completed the course		
	36 ran; 3 finished		

1952

1st	TEAL	(A.P.Thompson)	100/7
2nd	LEGAL JOY	(M.Scudamore)	100/6
3rd	WOT NO SUN	(D.V.Dick)	33/1
4th	UNCLE BARNEY	(J.Boddy)	100/1
	47 ran; 10 finished		

1953

1st	EARLY MIST	(B.Marshall)	20/1
2nd	MONT TREMBLANT	(D.V.Dick)	18/1
3rd	IRISH LIZARD	(R.Turnell)	33/1
4th	OVERSHADOW	(P.Taaffe)	33/1
	31 ran; 5 finished		

1956

1st	E.S.B.	(D.V.Dick)	100/7
2nd	GENTLE MOYA	(G.Milburn)	22/1
3rd	ROYAL TAN	(T.Taaffe)	28/1
4th	EAGLE LODGE	(A.Oughton)	66/1
	29 ran; 9 finished		

1957

1st	SUNDEW	(F.T.Winter)	20/1
2nd	WYNDBURGH	(M.Batchelor)	25/1
3rd	TIBERETTA	(A.Oughton)	66/1
4th	GLORIOUS TWELFTH	(B.Wilkinson)	100/8
	35 ran; 11 finished		

1958

1st	Mr What	(A.Freeman)	18/1
2nd	Tiberetta	(G.Slack)	28/1
3rd	Green Drill	(G.Milburn)	28/1
4th	Wyndburgh	(M.Batchelor)	6/1 Fav.
31 ran; 7 finished			

Mr What

1959

1st	Oxo	(M.Scudamore)	8/1
2nd	Wyndburgh	(T.Brookshaw)	10/1
3rd	Mr What	(T.Taaffe)	6/1 Fav.
4th	Tiberetta	(A.Oughton)	20/1
34 ran; 4 finished			

Oxo

1960

1st	Merryman II	(G.Scott)	13/2 Fav.
2nd	Badanloch	(S.Mellor)	100/7
3rd	Clear Profit	(B.Wilkinson)	20/1
4th	Tea Fiend	(P.G.Madden)	33/1
26 ran; 8 finished			

1961

1st	Nicolaus Silver	(H.R.Beasley)	28/1
2nd	Merryman II	(D.Ancil)	8/1
3rd	O'Malley Point	(P.A.Farrell)	100/6
4th	Scottish Flight II	(W.Rees)	100/6
35 ran; 14 finished			

Nicolaus Silver

1962

1st	Kilmore	(F.T.Winter)	28/1
2nd	Wyndburgh	(T.A.Barnes)	45/1
3rd	Mr What	(J.Lehane)	22/1
4th	Gay Navarree	(Mr A.Cameron)	100/1
32 ran; 17 finished			

1963

1st	Ayala	(P.Buckley)	66/1
2nd	Carrickbeg	(Mr J.Lawrence)	20/1
3rd	Hawa's Song	(P.Broderick)	28/1
4th	Team Spirit	(G.W.Robinson)	13/1
47 ran; 22 finished			

1964

1st	Team Spirit	(G.W.Robinson)	18/1
2nd	Purple Silk	(J.Kenneally)	100/6
3rd	Peacetown	(R.Edwards)	40/1
4th	Eternal	(Mr S.Davenport)	66/1
33 ran; 15 finished			

1965

1st	Jay Trump	(Mr T.C.Smith)	100/6
2nd	Freddie	(P.McCarron)	7/2 Fav.
3rd	Mr Jones	(Mr C.D.Collins)	50/1
4th	Rainbow Battle	(G.Milburn)	50/1
47 ran; 14 finished			

1966

1st	Anglo	(T.Norman)	50/1
2nd	Freddie	(P.McCarron)	11/4 Fav.
3rd	Forest Prince	(G.Scott)	100/7
4th	The Fossa	(T.W.Biddlecombe)	20/1
47 ran; 12 finished			

1967

1st	FOINAVON	(J.Buckingham)	100/1
2nd	HONEY END	(J.Gifford)	15/2 Fav.
3rd	RED ALLIGATOR	(B.Fletcher)	30/1
4th	GREEK SCHOLAR	(T.W.Biddlecombe)	20/1

44 ran; 18 finished

1968

1st	RED ALLIGATOR	(B.Fletcher)	100/7
2nd	MOIDORE'S TOKEN	(B.Brogan)	100/6
3rd	DIFFERENT CLASS	(D.Mould)	17/2 Fav.
4th	RUTHERFORDS	(P.Buckley)	100/9

45 ran; 17 finished

1969

1st	HIGHLAND WEDDING	(E.P.Harty)	100/9
2nd	STEEL BRIDGE	(R.Pitman)	50/1
3rd	RONDETTO	(J.King)	25/1
4th	THE BEECHES	(W.Rees)	100/6

30 ran; 14 finished

HIGHLAND WEDDING

1970

1st	GAY TRIP	(P.Taaffe)	15/1
2nd	VULTURE	(S.Barker)	15/1
3rd	MISS HUNTER	(F.Shortt)	33/1
4th	DOZO	(E.P.Harty)	100/8

28 ran; 7 finished

1971

1st	SPECIFY	(J.Cook)	28/1
2nd	BLACK SECRET	(Mr J.Dreaper)	20/1
3rd	ASTBURY	(J.Bourke)	33/1
4th	BOWGEENO	(G.Thorner)	66/1

38 ran; 13 finished

1972

1st	WELL TO DO	(G.Thorner)	14/1
2nd	GAY TRIP	(T.W.Biddlecombe)	12/1
★3rd	BLACK SECRET	(S.Barker)	14/1 ★Dead-heat
★3rd	GENERAL SYMONS	(P.Kiely)	40/1 ★Dead-heat

42 ran; 9 finished

1973

1st	RED RUM	(B.Fletcher)	9/1 Jnt/Fav.
2nd	CRISP	(R.Pitman)	9/1 Jnt/Fav.
3rd	L'ESCARGOT	(T.Carberry)	11/1
4th	SPANISH STEPS	(P.Blacker)	16/1

38 ran; 17 finished

1974

1st	RED RUM	(B.Fletcher)	11/1
2nd	L'ESCARGOT	(T.Carberry)	17/2
3rd	CHARLES DICKENS	(A.Turnell)	50/1
4th	SPANISH STEPS	(W.Smith)	15/1

42 ran; 17 finished

1975

1st	L'ESCARGOT	(T.Carberry)	13/2
2nd	RED RUM	(B.Fletcher)	7/2 Fav.
3rd	SPANISH STEPS	(W.Smith)	20/1
4th	MONEY MARKET	(J.King)	14/1

31 ran; 10 finished

1976

1st	RAG TRADE	(J.Burke)	14/1
2nd	RED RUM	(T.Stack)	10/1
3rd	EYECATCHER	(B.Fletcher)	28/1
4th	BARONA	(P.Kelleway)	7/1 Fav.

32 ran; 16 finished

1977

1st	RED RUM	(T.Stack)	9/1
2nd	CHURCHTOWN BOY	(M.Blackshaw)	20/1
3rd	EYECATCHER	(C.Read)	18/1
4th	THE PILGARLIC	(R.R.Evans)	40/1

42 ran; 11 finished

1978

1st	LUCIUS	(B.R.Davies)	14/1
2nd	SEBASTIAN V	(R.Lamb)	25/1
3rd	DRUMROAN	(G.Newman)	50/1
4th	COOLISHALL	(M.O'Halloran)	16/1

37 ran; 15 finished

1979

1st	RUBSTIC	(M.Barnes)	25/1
2nd	ZONGALERO	(B.R.Davies)	20/1
3rd	ROUGH AND TUMBLE	(J.Francome)	14/1
4th	THE PILGARLIC	(R.R.Evans)	16/1
34 ran; 7 finished			

RUBSTIC

1980

1st	BEN NEVIS	(Mr C.Fenwick)	40/1
2nd	ROUGH AND TUMBLE	(J.Francome)	11/1
3rd	THE PILGARLIC	(R.Hyett)	33/1
4th	ROYAL STUART	(P.Blacker)	20/1
30 ran; 4 finished			

BEN NEVIS

1981

1st	ALDANITI	(R.Champion)	10/1
2nd	SPARTAN MISSILE	(Mr M J.Thorne)	8/1 Fav.
3rd	ROYAL MAIL	(P.Blacker)	16/1
4th	THREE TO ONE	(Mr T.G.Dun)	33/1
39 ran; 12 finished			

1982

1st	GRITTAR	(Mr C.R.Saunders)	7/1 Fav.
2nd	HARD OUTLOOK	(A.Webber)	50/1
3rd	LOVING WORDS	(R.Hoare)	16/1 (remounted)
4th	DELMOSS	(W.Smith)	50/1
39 ran; 8 finished			

1983

1st	CORBIERE	(B.De Haan)	13/1
2nd	GREASEPAINT	(Mr C.Magnier)	14/1
3rd	YER MAN	(T.V.O'Connell)	80/1
4th	HALLO DANDY	(N.Doughty)	60/1
41 ran; 10 finished			

1984

1st	HALLO DANDY	(N.Doughty)	13/1
2nd	GREASEPAINT	(T.Carmody)	9/1 Fav.
3rd	CORBIERE	(B.De Haan)	16/1
4th	LUCKY VANE	(J.Burke)	12/1
40 ran; 23 finished			

1985

1st	LAST SUSPECT	(H.Davies)	50/1
2nd	MR SNUGFIT	(P.Tuck)	12/1
3rd	CORBIERE	(P.Scudamore)	9/1
4th	GREASEPAINT	(T.Carmody)	13/2 Jnt/Fav.
40 ran; 11 finished			

1986

1st	WEST TIP	(R.Dunwoody)	15/2
2nd	YOUNG DRIVER	(C.Grant)	66/1
3rd	CLASSIFIED	(S.Smith Eccles)	22/1
4th	MR SNUGFIT	(P.Tuck)	13/2 Fav.
40 ran; 17 finished			

1987

1st	MAORI VENTURE	(S.C.Knight)	28/1
2nd	THE TSAREVICH	(J.White)	20/1
3rd	LEAN AR AGHAIDH	(G.Landau)	14/1
4th	WEST TIP	(R.Dunwoody)	5/1 Fav.
40 ran; 22 finished			

MAORI VENTURE

1988

1st	RHYME 'N' REASON	(B.Powell)	10/1
2nd	DURHAM EDITION	(C.Grant)	20/1
3rd	MONANORE	(T.J.Taaffe)	33/1
4th	WEST TIP	(R.Dunwoody)	11/1
	40 ran; 9 finished		

1989

1st	LITTLE POLVEIR	(J.Frost)	28/1
2nd	WEST TIP	(R.Dunwoody)	12/1
3rd	THE THINKER	(S.Sherwood)	10/1
4th	LASTOFTHEBROWNIES	(T.Carmody)	16/1
	40 ran; 14 finished		

LITTLE POLVEIR

1990

1st	MR FRISK	(Mr M.Armytage)	16/1
2nd	DURHAM EDITION	(C.Grant)	9/1
3rd	RINUS	(N.Doughty)	13/1
4th	BROWN WINDSOR	(J.White)	7/1 Fav.
	38 ran; 20 finished		

1991

1st	SEAGRAM	(N.Hawke)	12/1
2nd	GARRISON SAVANNAH	(M.Pitman)	7/1
3rd	AUNTIE DOT	(M.Dwyer)	50/1
4th	OVER THE ROAD	(R.Supple)	50/1
	40 ran; 17 finished		

1992

1st	PARTY POLITICS	(C.Llewellyn)	14/1
2nd	ROMANY KING	(R.Guest)	16/1
3rd	LAURA'S BEAU	(C.O'Dwyer)	12/1
4th	DOCKLANDS EXPRESS	(P.Scudamore)	15/2 Fav.
	40 ran; 22 finished		

1993

RACE VOID

1994

1st	MIINNEHOMA	(R.Dunwoody)	16/1
2nd	JUST SO	(S.Burrough)	20/1
3rd	MOORCROFT BOY	(A.Maguire)	5/1 Fav.
4th	EBONY JANE	(L.Cusack)	25/1
	36 ran; 6 finished		

1995

1st	ROYAL ATHLETE	(J.Titley)	40/1
2nd	PARTY POLITICS	(M.Dwyer)	16/1
3rd	OVER THE DEEL	(Mr C.Bonner)	100/1
4th	DUBACILLA	(D.Gallagher)	9/1
	35 ran; 15 finished		

ROYAL ATHLETE

1996

1st	ROUGH QUEST	(M.Fitzgerald)	7/1 Fav.
2nd	ENCORE UN PEU	(D.Bridgwater)	14/1
3rd	SUPERIOR FINISH	(R.Dunwoody)	9/1
4th	SIR PETER LELY	(Mr C.Bonner)	33/1
	27 ran; 17 finished		

1997

1st	LORD GYLLENE	(A.Dobbin)	14/1
2nd	SUNY BAY	(J.Osborne)	8/1
3rd	CAMELOT KNIGHT	(C.Llewellyn)	100/1
4th	BUCKBOARD BOUNCE	(P.Carberry)	40/1
	36 ran; 17 finished		

1998

1st	EARTH SUMMIT	(C.Llewellyn)	7/1 Fav.
2nd	SUNY BAY	(G.Bradley)	11/1
3rd	SAMLEE	(R.Dunwoody)	8/1
4th	ST MELLION FAIRWAY	(A.Thornton)	20/1
	37 ran; 6 finished		

1999

1st	BOBBYJO	(P.Carberry)	10/1
2nd	BLUE CHARM	(L.Wyer)	25/1
3rd	CALL IT A DAY	(R.Dunwoody)	7/1
4th	ADDINGTON BOY	(A.Maguire)	10/1
	32 ran; 18 finished		

2000

1st	PAPILLON	(R.Walsh)	10/1
2nd	MELY MOSS	(N.Williamson)	25/1
3rd	NIKI DEE	(R.Supple)	25/1
4th	BRAVE HIGHLANDER	(P.Hide)	50/1
	40 ran; 17 finished		

INDEX

Entries in *italics* refer to pictures.

Design and repro by Prima Creative Services

Printed in Italy

AUTHOR'S ACKNOWLEDGEMENTS

My heartfelt thanks are extended to photographers Alan Johnson and Colin Turner whose work I have long admired.
The *Racing Post* and *Liverpool Echo* have always provided a reliable source of information for which I am also grateful.
It is a personal delight that artist Ian Carter has, at late notice, supplied a number of his 'Classic National Winners' to enhance the pictorial content of this work.
As always I am indebted to Aintree racecourse itself for providing me with over 50 years of unforgettable memories. I congratulate its management and staff for restoring the Grand National to its rightful place in the sporting world.
Finally and most sincerely, I thank my editor Jonathan Taylor for his patience and tolerance and for keeping me on-course and well balanced at every obstacle throughout a lengthy though thoroughly memorable journey.

PICTURE CREDITS

© **Ian Carter:** 81, 97 and all images in the Race Results section
© **Alan Johnson:** 22/23, 65
© **Colin Turner:** 46 (bottom), 47 (both), 55, 60, 136/137, 141, 142 (both), 143
© **Allsport:** 86, 106, 122
© **Hulton Getty:** 118, 119, 135 (top)
© **Kris Photography:** 40/41
All other images © **Reg Green/National Scene and Aintree Racecourse Limited**